In Search of the Kingdom

Private Faith, Public Discipleship

Patrick Woodhouse

Marshall Pickering

B44/07

For
Hannah and Imogen.

Marshall Morgan and Scott
Marshall Pickering
34–42 Cleveland Street, London W1P 5FB, U.K.

Copyright © 1989 Patrick Woodhouse

First published in 1989 by Marshall Morgan and Scott Publications
Ltd
Part of the Marshall Pickering Holdings Group

British Library CIP Data
Woodhouse, Patrick
    In search of the kingdom.
    1. Christian life. Faith
    I. Title
    248.4

    ISBN: 0–551–01877–1

Phototypeset by Input Typesetting Ltd, London
Printed in Great Britain by Cox and Wyman, Reading

Acknowledgement is due to Oxford University Press for permission to
use an extract from Christopher Fry's play *A Sleep of Prisoners*, OUP,
1951.

CONTENTS

PART TWO

IN SEARCH OF OUR SELVES

FOREWORD

Perhaps the most difficult task confronting the Christian church today is that of recovering, or creating, a coherent vision of what the Christian religion is about – a revisioning of faith. It is a slow, and at times, an agonising process, which demands a truthfulness, courage and intelligence that at times seems beyond us. We can only reject blind certainties, move hesitantly, try out thoughts and ideas and approaches, be warm and generous to those who try new things.

What I like about Patrick Woodhouse's book is that it takes some positive steps in revisioning, in particular in showing concern for the 'innerness' of faith. There are many to whom faith is primarily concerned with externals, with observing rituals and following ethical guide-lines, but who do not have any sense of 'journey' or seem to need to experience God for themselves. Patrick Woodhouse is not like that. Weaving material both from his own life and from the life of Thomas Merton he asks some pertinent questions about 'innerness'. He considers where the Christian religion comes from and, in terms of the interface of political ideology and theology, where we are going to. Like many thinking Christians today he uses the insights of psychotherapy.

What I like best about the book is that instead of seeing faith as a possession, like a portfolio of promising equities over which one might gloat smugly, Patrick Woodhouse thinks of it more in terms of a sort of joyous struggling – what a musician I know of, speaking of the effort of composition, calls 'passionate argument'. If we think of the Christian religion as a sort of creativity, with ourselves, under God, struggling to create the world in the image of love, then each of us has the task of the artist. The process of creation may be much more contradictory, intractable and confusing than, in our naïveté, we once supposed, yet it is that sort of fascinating and surprising learning process that the religious life is all about. Patrick Woodhouse's book will give us valuable clues on how to proceed.

MONICA FURLONG

PREFACE

The suggestion that I write this book came entirely out of the blue, and I am grateful to Christine Whitell of Marshall Pickering for pushing me in the first place. Without her initial confidence, it is quite certain that nothing would have appeared at all

My indebtedness to the ideas and writings of others who have explored far more deeply than I have these three areas of biblical scholarship, personal conversion and social responsibility – the subjects of the three parts of this search – will be apparent on almost every page. There are detailed references at the back of the book for those who would like to explore further among the writers that I have cited. My concern has been to share something of my own experience of faith as a search; a search which is rooted in the biblical story, travels through the difficult terrain of personal faith and doubt, and emerges into the public realm – the area where the Church finds discipleship so difficult, and yet where the questions about what it means to believe, press upon us so urgently.

In all this, I am enormously grateful to many people: particularly, to friends in the Diocese of Winchester for their support and the discussion we share together; to Dr Zaida Hall of the Psychotherapy Department of the Royal South Hants Hospital for her encouraging response to a draft of Part 2; to Professor Raymond Plant of Southampton University whose work on the ideology of Conservative Capitalism has been immensely helpful to me personally as well as to many others in the Church in Britain; I am grateful to him for commenting on a draft of Part 3, and for his friendship and support; to Brother

Bernard of the Society of Saint Francis who took time to read a draft of the whole manuscript, and pushed me further; to the Franciscan community at Hilfield Friary and the Sisters of Bethany at Winchester, for their generous hospitality at various times. I would also like to express thanks to the Bishop and colleagues in the Diocese of Winchester who enabled me to take a period of study leave in the summer of 1988, and to June Harding, Christine Simmonds and Jane Miall for their help at various stages in the typing. Finally, I am most grateful to Monica Furlong for her interest and kindness in writing the Foreword.

My gratitude to my wife Sam, is of a different order. Without her encouragement, confidence and understanding, not only would this book never have seen the light of day, but my own understanding of the search of faith would be immeasurably poorer.

Patrick Woodhouse
February 1989.

INTRODUCTION:
Faith as a Search

So I saw him and sought him; I had him and wanted him. It seems to me that this is and should be an experience common to us all.
                    Julian of Norwich

What does it mean to be a Christian in this society as we come towards the end of the twentieth century? This book is an attempt to explore that question. Let me say straight away that I do not find it an easy question and I'm quite sure that there is no easy answer. That's why it helps to think of faith in terms of a *search* — a search for the Kingdom of God coming 'here on earth as in heaven'. The imminent arrival of the Kingdom was, as we shall see in Chapter 2, *the* central idea in Jesus' life and mission. But he often spoke of it in terms of a search — it is therefore an appropriate way for us to think too.

But I have a more personal reason for wanting to see faith in these terms. It is quite simply because that's what the life of faith *feels* like for me most of the time. How can I describe what I mean? Like most believers, I don't find faith easy; it feels like a struggle, a constant struggle to break through the surface of life and find the God whom I believe in, but seem constantly to be losing touch with. God, and the experience of God feels for me very *elusive* — out of reach. I search for him and I can't find him and though I still believe, the unspoken cry is 'Where are You?' It is a cry that comes from a sense of restlessness, emptiness and the conviction that life is more than the shallow and rather agitated busy-ness that I so often feel trapped in.

This sense of the loss of God can, of course, come in far worse situations than just the routine busy-ness that we get caught up in. Suddenly something happens that blows our world to bits — a death or sudden tragedy. At such a moment a person's structure of meaning can be shattered like a pane of glass. In an instant the world is drained of any hope, or love, or God, and the cry 'Where are You?' is anguished. Chasms of emptiness have been opened up inside. Few of us experience that kind of emptiness, or if we do we learn to defend ourselves against it — we feel it cannot be lived with. However, paradoxically, such experience can offer a hard way through to the ground and foundation of a deep faith. We shall look more carefully at this strange paradox in the second part of the book when we come to explore the personal search for the Kingdom.

But for most of us, most of the time, our sense of emptiness is more commonplace and ordinary. We are simply conscious of restlessness and agitated activity, and the grasping at distractions that we sense are some kind of protection against the inner question. At all costs we must keep our lives moving . . .

But it is not always like that. There are moments when the searching ends and we do 'find', times when we break through to deeper trust and sharing with others and discover what the great American theologian Paul Tillich called 'The Depth of Existence'.[1] This experience may come in all kinds of ways: through shared sorrow or grief, or honest anger, or intellectual struggle. But mostly it comes — is given — in and through the experience of loving; loving as mutual vulnerability and profound acceptance — the kind of loving that yields joy.

These are the moments when we 'find'— when the surface of life is breached and we touch the depth in ourselves and others where God is. In this experience something happens. Often it is a sense of being able to see again — like coming out of a fog. We re-engage in the process of life itself, the world is illuminated, options are clarified, we find we are able to care, and life is injected with new meaning and fresh energy to continue the action, the direction, the dance of faith.

However, such occasions of 'depth' can be comparatively

rare, and it is not long before we find ourselves dragged back to the business of survival at the surface where anxiety, fear and the need to succeed are the constant enslaving impulses. We are back with the struggle to believe and find God again, who somehow we have lost. This is what discipleship so often feels like.

It is reassuring to find this experience mirrored in the New Testament. Jesus repeatedly used this image of the search in his stories about the Kingdom — faith pictured as a search for something which is lost. One of those stories was about a coin. The Kingdom of God, he said, is like a woman who lost a coin — one of ten very valuable coins. She was poor and this coin mattered a great deal. She searched her home from top to bottom. At long last, after she had turned the place upside down, she suddenly found it. She was so overjoyed that she called in friends and neighbours, and so we get the refrain in the Gospels: 'Rejoice with me for that which is lost is found'(Luke 15:8–10).

I imagine her rushing out of her small Palestinian house into the narrow street shouting her delight, banging on her neighbours doors. Perhaps she gathered the other housewives in and the lost precious coin was put in a special place. I imagine them sitting together laughing and joking as she told the story of the search and shared what the coin meant.

The same story is told in different terms a few verses earlier. This time it's a shepherd who has lost just one sheep out of the flock. Again this sheep matters a lot for the shepherd leaves the whole of the rest of the flock to find this lost one (Luke 15:4–7). Not knowing the Palestinian hills, I like to imagine the story in terms of the Cumbrian fells. Up goes the shepherd into the rain and mist stumbling over the wet slippery rocks. Where is this sheep? It must be found. Every so often as he climbs higher he stops to listen. Not a sound. Nothing but the damp eerie silence of the wet hills. He climbs higher, and then after several hours of combing the fell side, faintly in the distance he hears the tiniest bleating coming from an outcrop of rock. He scrambles the last few yards and there it is, sodden and shivering with cold. Gently he picks it up, places it across his shoulders and begins the long descent. 'When he got home' said Jesus 'would he not call in his friends and neighbours saying "Rejoice with me for I have found my sheep which was lost?" '

A third search story is about a merchant who is searching for fine pearls and comes across one of very special value (Matthew 13:45). The punch line here is not so much in the note of rejoicing as in the cost of possessing it. He immediately goes off and sells everything he has, including all his other pearls, simply in order to take possession of this one magnificent pearl.

From coins to sheep to pearls to people. The best known story of search is the story of the prodigal or lost son (Luke 15:11–32). Here the element of search is expressed through the waiting and longing of the Father. The son demands his share of the property and is off into the far country. Months go by. No news. The Father is desolate as he waits. Day after day he scans the empty road, searching in his mind for some understanding as to why the boy should suddenly take off. At last one day, he sees a figure in the distance — dishevelled, head down, almost unrecognisable. The Father, says Jesus, runs to the boy, 'clasps him in his arms and kisses him tenderly.' He's not interested in apologies, or expressions of remorse, or resolutions to do better. All that matters is that the waiting and the searching is over. The boy is back and as they return to the farm, the shout of delight is the same: 'Rejoice with me, that which is lost is found!'

In these searching and finding stories, the punch line is almost always at the end in the note of jubilation and celebration and in the reuniting with that which was lost — the atonement. But the stories are also saying something about the *process of faith itself*; that faith is not a matter of gaining instant access to the life of God, but involves a long and often costly search, a search which will take time, energy and sustained commitment. The New Testament itself begins with such a search: the long and diligent search of the three astrologers who came 'from the east' — following the star in search of the infant King. The story, as it has developed through Christmas legend, is of a long trek over desert mountains and plains following the star. It is appropriate for the good news of the Kingdom of God to begin in this way for Jesus makes it plain later in that same gospel that the way to the Kingdom is not easy. The road he said is 'narrow' and those who find it are few, though they may be the few who bring salvation — the few grains of yeast that leaven the whole dough.

Faith then is searching. Hard, costly, committed searching — though it is also the incomparable joy of finding! This is our theme. This is what we shall explore. In this process the New Testament is clear that we do not search alone. Not only is the search something to be shared in company with others — indeed should be· the very life of the Church — but also according to Paul, God Himself searches with us. In his first letter to the Corinthians, he writes of 'the Spirit who explores everything, even the depths of God's own nature . . . this is the Spirit we have received' (1 Cor 2:10). Searching then is at the very heart of God, and therefore is at the very heart of faith.

My hope is that this book may be an encouragement for some to engage more deeply in this search, and for others perhaps to begin afresh. However, as we contemplate setting out, there are, at the risk of over-simplification, two immediate dangers. One is that in recognising that the task is difficult, we quickly assume it is hopeless, abandon it, and surrender to a kind of mild, unspoken and perhaps well-masked despair, and float with the surface of life seeking whatever kind of pleasure and distraction we may, in a world without reference points and ultimately without meaning. The second temptation is the opposite and one that Christians seem particularly prone to, and it is perhaps even worse; it is to assume that there really is no searching of any depth to be done at all; that we have already found the treasure of the Kingdom, and the task is simply to proclaim it. All too easily this kind of approach leads to a superficial spirituality and an over zealous commitment that serves as a cloak under which to conceal any number of unresolved personal hang-ups.

If we can find our way between these two poles, the temptation to despair fed by the suspicion that the whole religious enterprise is a great protective illusion, and the temptation to pretend that we have found when we know in our hearts that we have not, then we shall, to use another biblical image of faith, be on the journey — a journey of search into a promised future.

But what are we after? What is this 'promised future'? At one level, the answer may seem simple enough: 'Seek first' said Jesus, 'the Kingdom of God' (Luke 12:31). However that simply begs the question. What is this 'Kingdom of God'? What does this phrase *mean* in terms of our experience? It may be said that as and when we 'find' we shall simply 'know', and the phrase the 'Kingdom of God' will take on very personal and specific meaning for us as we experience moments of the presence of God that are 'given'. This is of course true. Let's pause here and reflect. Can you identify particular moments of 'the Kingdom' in your experience? I think of a group of parents on a bleak estate in the north of England coming together through the efforts of a Community Development Worker, breaking through to a level of trust they had not previously known, and pressing the District Council to provide a new Community Centre, and then having a grand party to celebrate the day it was opened by the bishop! I think of simple moments of sheer delight in my family when the children have pierced barriers of adult pretentiousness! I think of sharing in personal conversation in a pub with a friend and finding a rare degree of mutual trust and vulnerability. I think of the silence of shared worship and then the simple tune of a Taizé song, sung over and over again in meditative praying in a Franciscan friary spilling over into a profound sense of being at one before God. I think of odd disturbing flashes of understanding — moments when I have become aware of a profound fragility and weakness, a sense of finitude and the reality of death — and then by way of contrast, glimpsing and knowing the sheer softness and miracle and gift of life itself . . . that I AM at all! Moments of the Kingdom, very ordinary moments, when the life and reign of God is glimpsed. One more example from the experience of Bishop Simeon Nkoane of Johannesburg recounted in a recent lecture on spirituality in situations of conflict. He tells of visiting, together with Desmond Tutu and another bishop, the bereaved wife of one of his clergy:

> I was with the Bishop of Zululand and the then Bishop Tutu and we went to express our condolences to a bereaved minister's wife. After the greeting formalities, Bishop Tutu began singing:
>
> > Nge gazi le mvana
> > Nge gazi le mvana
> > Nge gazi le mvana
> > siya sindiswa
>
> > By the blood of the lamb
> > By the blood of the lamb
> > By the blood of the lamb
> > We shall be saved.
>
> We sang the chorus several times over and in that moment we were led to the root of our being where we encountered the Lord and our departed colleague and found each other and the widow and were strengthened
> by
> the unity won for us through Christ's reconciling blood.[2]

It's a powerful description of a very ordinary scene of pastoral care — but transformed; there is given a strengthening, a profound unity and an experience of finding one another at 'the root of our being'. Is not this to enter into the Kingdom of God?

The characteristics of such experiences are so often, vulnerability, trust and a breakthrough to a new level of *seeing* — i.e. vision, and to a depth of *belonging* — an at-one-ness with one another and the Ground of Life itself. And yet such elusive and occasional glimpses cannot provide the basis of faith. To pin hope on such fleeting moments is to have no clear direction and to be stranded indeed when inspiration simply dries up. Such moments may be comforting and even deeply sustaining, but we do know *more* than just illuminating moments of personal and corporate experience however valuable they may be. The phrase 'the Kingdom of God' has specific content in and through the biblical tradition. This will be our focus in the first part of the book.

First in the Old Testament we are given the story of a people who set out in search of a promise. Through this promise and their search for it, they believed they were uniquely shown the nature of this Kingdom and the character of God the King. In the New Testament, the claim is that the Kingdom is brought through the life, death and resurrection of the Jew, Jesus of Nazareth, right into the middle of our world and offered to us as pure gift; the potential for a new creation right in the middle of the old one. This is what has been given to us and any search for the Kingdom in our world must begin with it, if we are to guard against a rudderless wandering based solely on our own experience.

In Part One I ask two questions. First, what understandings of the Reign of God can we see in the Hebrew story — are there particular *Jewish* ways of thinking about the Kingdom? Second, what did the Kingdom of God mean in the life and teaching of the Jew, Jesus of Nazareth — and what does it mean to say that he brings this Kingdom into our world? In sketching the answer to these I have drawn on the work of those far more learned than I am, and it is certainly not easy to summarise such large areas in just two chapters. Nevertheless, I believe it to be possible and necessary to try to present as succinctly as possible the fundamentals of the Hebrew hope as we know it from the Old Testament, and the good news of the Kingdom as we know it from the first three Gospels, even if it is only in brief outline. We need to grasp that which is the basic *data* (i.e. that which is given) of the Kingdom which can be taken up and used in our own specific contemporary searchings. Unless this data is clarified our search is rootless, and the words 'the Kingdom of God' can come to mean anything we wish them to mean, or nothing much at all.

In Part Two and Part Three I ask, what may the search for the Kingdom lead us into in our *personal faith* (Part Two) and our *social responsibility* (Part Three)? Here the search really begins. We have the gospel of Jesus Christ rooted in the Jewish tradition and interpreted by Mark, Luke, Matthew, John and Paul and the other writers of the New Testament, writing out of their particular historical circumstances. That's the foundation. Built on this is the experience of twenty centuries of Christian tradition, the background of any contemporary personal and corporate search. All this is given and we constantly draw on it. But the questions remain: (a) how may I personally enter more deeply into this experience of the Life of God? And (b) what might it mean to go in search of the Kingdom in our particular society at this particular time? A personal and a social question. It is important to underline that the two are, of course, inextricably linked. The Kingdom is not just about personal liberation — it is fundamentally a corporate and ultimately a universal symbol. The division between the personal and the political that bedevils Christian mission is an illusion.

Finally, I have tried in a brief 'Epilogue' to focus the questions for the Church that I can see leading out of all this. This is the area that I find the most difficult, and where so much more work needs to be done and deeper praying and thinking is required. For the Christian the Church must be our home and life — it is where the Gospel is read and the Eucharist celebrated. And yet again and again, I hear of friends and acquaintances who, seeking to be faithful to their understanding of the Kingdom, despair over the Church and feel constantly to be on the edge of it. Could this be a sign not so much of their failure but of their faithfulness? In his biography of Bishop John Robinson, Eric James writes of Robinson quoting approvingly the words of a student: 'We must try to be at one and the same time *for* the Church and *against* the Church. They alone can serve her faithfully whose consciences are continually exercised as to whether they ought not for Christ's sake, to leave her.'[3] In the context of this study the question is simply this: are there ways by which the Church may more faithfully point to the Kingdom and embody the character of the Kingdom? In all this it would be foolish to attempt easy answers. We are in search of a Church that will more faithfully search out and nourish the Life of the Kingdom in the individual believer, in society, and in the life of the community of the church. There is no blueprint for our search. We simply need to seek the next step in the right direction. My hope is that this book will assist that movement.

The book is wide-ranging and necessarily brief. What I believe is important, is that in a Church riven by competing groups claiming that their particular emphasis is the right way, we need to try to understand the Kingdom in terms of a search that will and must take us all into the unfamiliar and the unknown. This becomes a central theme particularly as we examine, in Part Two, Thomas Merton's story which is a kind of paradigm of searching faith in the twentieth century. He teaches us, above all, that if we are seriously in search of the promised Kingdom of God, then like the people of Israel themselves, we shall have to go into the unknown — into the desert. In this travelling, we must take with us every emphasis and understanding gained thus far: both those which are briefly explored in this book and others only touched on here. For the Kingdom of God is both Jewish *and* Christian, personal *and* political, contemplative *and* active, to be found in the church *and* beyond the church, within our grasp — and beyond all our understandings.

We are in search of the Kingdom. Where do we begin? The first part of the book points towards basic definitions but not in any generalised or abstract way. Always the Kingdom is shared in and through the lives of individuals and communities by means of stories. Two stories are fundamental: the story of the Hebrews and the story of Jesus. To that first story we now turn.

PART ONE

IN SEARCH OF OUR ROOTS

One has either got to be a Jew or stop reading the Bible.
Thomas Merton

Chapter 1: A People in Search

The Hebrew story that begins with Abraham presents us with the ultimate model for faith as a search. As we grasp the outline of their physical journey and movement forward — particularly in the story of the Exodus: the break-out from Egypt, the painful learning to risk and trust for food and drink and life one day at a time, the giving of the law, the desert wanderings, and eventually the entry into the promised land . . . as we grasp this and get a sense of the dust in their throats, and the continual march under a desert sun towards an unknown horizon, what becomes clear — at first only dimly and in fragments — are the features and emerging characteristics of this rule and reign of Yahweh their God. As they followed the promise of the land in blind and often resentful obedience, they learnt amidst the harsh rigours of the desert the ways and purposes of this holy sovereign God who no ordinary man could come close to or see, and they came to trust in his constant care. He was always with them and yet always ahead of them leading them forward in search of the promise into ever harsher emptiness.

This is the story, with its sense of ever forward movement, which provides the fundamental shape of all searching faith as well as the backcloth and context for the second story, the story of Jesus of Nazareth. It also gives us clues to the nature and progress of our own individual stories which will be the focus of Part Two. Through the Hebrew story and the story of Jesus, and the relationship between them, we are given the basic *data* of the Kingdom of God. These stories lay the foundations without which any talk of the Kingdom is shapeless, and can fall prey to the tyranny of any number of ideologies.

Jesus the Jew

Before coming to look at this story more closely, a simple question presents itself: Why is the Jewish story so important? Church people may well ask: doesn't *Christian* faith begin with the proclamation, death and resurrection of Jesus and the life of the early Church? Why then such an emphasis upon the *Jews*? Of course it is important — some may say — to be tolerant of all religions, and all civilised Christian people are appalled by the horrors of the holocaust, but nevertheless, is it not true, that the Christian story and revelation has spelt the end of the special significance of the Jews? Put bluntly, has not the old covenant for the Jews been superseded by the new covenant of Jesus Christ which is for *all*— Jew and Gentile alike — and so the proper place to begin any search for the Kingdom must be with Jesus?

This approach fails to reckon with the fact that Jesus of Nazareth lived and died as a Jew, an inheritor and upholder of the tradition of the law and the prophets, and like the prophets who were stoned, abused and persecuted before him, faithful to the very deepest and greatest strand of that tradition.

Of course Christians will want to say that Jesus was more than a prophet, and to that we shall come in the next chapter. But whatever the claims the Church may make about him, if we are to have any chance of understanding the teaching of Jesus about the Kingdom, and enter into the experience he offers *of* the Kingdom, it is with the Jews that we must begin, for *he* was a Jew — a vine nurtured in the soil of Jewish experience and Jewish understandings of God, formed over the long history of their search. They were his understandings too. We who have attached ourselves through baptism and membership of the church to Jesus Christ — as branches of that vine — must also draw strength and nourishment and a sense of direction from the roots of the same tree that he did, and they are *Jewish* roots — *our* roots. Any search for the Kingdom of God which Jesus proclaimed must therefore begin with some attempt to learn from the Jews.

Unlearning and relearning

However, even to face the question of looking as clearly as possible at the Jewish story, and distinctively Jewish perceptions of God, is enormously difficult for Christians, for over the centuries a severance from these life-giving roots has taken place. In his book *True God*, Kenneth Leech describes this cutting-off in terms of a challenge to a fundamental re-education as to what faith is about:

> Much Christian theology, including much biblical study, has helped to sever the links between the Old and New Testaments, thus disconnecting the history of Israel from that of the Christian Church. The severance has formed the basis for a whole pathology in which materialism and spirituality, politics and prayer, are seen as opposites. To turn from such a deranged spiritual tradition to the faith of Israel, the faith of *our* fathers, is to begin the painful process of unlearning, and relearning what religion is about.[1]

It has also of course, been more than a severance. The separate faiths (for that is now how they are seen) have not amicably agreed to go their separate ways. The tragic truth is that over the centuries the Church has turned on the Jews, and both initiated and shared in the most violent and bitter persecution. We have portrayed them as nothing less than the murderers of God, instead of the heirs and upholders of the tradition that uniquely *reveals* God. It is an extraordinary reversal of the truth which has led to the most appalling consequences. The German theologian Jürgen Moltmann writes:

> Auschwitz was to be 'the final solution' of the 'Jewish question'. The Jewish question, however, existed already for 2000 years inasmuch as Jewish existence was brought

into question by the Christian church and the Christian empire. Auschwitz is the end-point of a long anti-Jewish development in Christianity . . . the process of rethinking must lead to a rethinking of Christianity at its very roots.[2]

The very ugly truth has been that instead of honouring them and their tradition, seeking to learn from them as our ancestors in the faith, and seeing in those who crucified and denied Jesus simply ourselves writ large, we have used them to carry our guilt and shame, scapegoated them, turned on them, and depicted their whole tradition as flawed and in error. The Collect for Good Friday in the *Book of Common Prayer* which has moulded the minds of generations of Anglican worshippers reads:

> O merciful God, who hast made all men, and hatest nothing that thou hast made, nor wouldest the death of a sinner, but rather that he should be converted and live; have mercy upon all Jews, Turks, Infidels, and Hereticks, and take from them all ignorance, hardness of heart, and contempt of thy Word; and so fetch them home, blessed Lord, to thy flock, that they may be saved among the remnant of the true Israelites, and be made one fold under one shepherd, Jesus Christ our Lord, who liveth and reigneth with thee and the Holy Spirit, one God, world without end.

In the new *Alternative Service Book*, astonishingly the note of arrogance and plain anti-semitism remains:

> Merciful God,
> who made all men and hate nothing that you have made:
> you desire not the death of a sinner
> but rather that he should be converted and live.
> Have mercy upon your ancient people the Jews,
> and upon all who have not known you,
> or who deny the faith of Christ crucified;
> take from them all ignorance, hardness of heart,

and contempt for your Word,
and so fetch them home to your fold
that they may be made one flock under one shepherd;
through Jesus Christ our Lord.

It is an extraordinary prayer which has survived liturgical revision into the new Anglican prayer book. There is the clear implication that God may just 'hate' the Jews. Secondly, the implicit suggestion, on Good Friday, that it is of course the Jews — and just the Jews — who killed Jesus. And thirdly, it explicitly assumes that the Jews — though God's 'ancient people' — have never known him, and are ignorant, hard-hearted and contemptuous of the Word of God. Psychiatrists will tell us that it has been convenient to be able to portray the Jews in this way: they have become the receptacle for the disowned and split-off darker side of human nature which we can then punish in them. These prayers, faithfully prayed by generations of Christian worshippers are simply a sign of the hatred and mistrust that has gone very deep and all of us who have been bred in the Christian tradition are likely to have these seeds within us. Ask yourself as honestly as you can: *What do you think of the Jews?* What kind of prejudice is buried in your heart?

I find this a searching question. The school I went to had a House especially set aside for the Jews. During those formative years I had the opportunity at first hand to sense something of this Christian-Jewish dissonance. On the surface, there wasn't much to notice: while maintaining their separate identity, the Jews joined in fully in the life of the school. There were many friendships and we lived and worked and played games together. However underneath you could not escape the difference; a difference marked on our side by some feeling of suspicion and resentment. What was it that we resented about them? I suppose at one level it was that they were just different — and set out to be so. In any school, any minority that quite deliberately decides to live out its difference, even when the school officially sanctions and applauds that difference is bound to incur some resentment from the majority. But it was more than just being a dissenting minority: it was the *way* they were different. They looked different, many of them still håving distinctive Jewish features. They dressed differently — or at least better. All of us were obliged to wear the uniform of the school, a grey suit, but the Jewish boys I particularly knew and sat next to somehow had the most beautiful suits. They seemed conspicuously rich too. At Commemoration Day parents of the Jewish boys would arrive in large expensive cars. Perhaps it was their obvious success and ability that we resented for they consistently carried off school trophies in certain areas. In itself none of this amounted to much, and may seem rather trivial, and there were no doubt scruffy light-skinned members of the Jewish House who stumbled along like the rest of us half succeeding and half not, and conspicuous for nothing in particular. And yet I suspect that in microcosm the experience in that school revealed much of what the 'Jewish question' was about.

It was on Saturdays — their Sabbath — that the difference really became clear. While we attended lessons they were nowhere to be seen. Suddenly the Jews you had sat next to all week in the classroom had vanished, their desks empty as they kept their Sabbath, worshipping in their synagogue. What became startlingly clear on Saturdays was that they were committed to their religion in a way that somehow we were not. It was central to their identity and they were living it out week by week by their Sabbath observance. Their religion seemed to belong to them in a way that ours somehow never did.

The religion that we were obliged to observe through compulsory Chapel attendance every morning as well as Sundays was a kind of public affair that belonged to anybody and nobody. As we shuffled morning by morning into the vast gaunt circular Chapel, it had a parade-ground mentality about it. Always on the door stood the school 'Marshall' — a sort of policeman — looking us over to see who needed a haircut. When the dark brown pews had been filled with row upon row of snuffling teenage boys, the place went silent and in through the West Door marched the *Praeposters*, two abreast, swinging their arms, heels hitting the floor in time, with the Head Boy bringing up the rear. At first sight, as a new boy, it was rather awe-inspiring and I guess most of us secretly aspired to this position of being able to march in every morning in silence with six-hundred pairs of eyes focused on you. Then after the Headmaster in black gown had taken his large canopied seat, the Chaplain would begin the service. By this daily ritual, there was drilled into us that sense of order and hierarchy and discipline, and above all service to the nation (there were constant prayers for the Queen and the Royal Family and the 'High Court of Parliament') that was no doubt regarded as fundamental to the British way of life and our place within it. It wasn't all negative. In its own rather dreary and colourless way it was even comforting — giving us a sense of belonging to something bigger than ourselves that was all tied up with a rather distant God. But, I fear that that 'something' was at heart the British way of life and the British way of doing things, and as young members of the professional class we were being drilled into the particular responsibilities of leadership.

Whilst we paraded and droned our half-hearted way through Anglican hymns and chants, with vigorous hymn practices on Saturdays and visiting preachers and bishops on Sundays, the Jews worshipped secretly in their basement. Their separateness somehow made them special and we knew — without being able to put it into words — that that claim to be special, rested on a *divine* call and a *divine* choice: they were the *chosen* people and this lay, I suspect, at the root of our unarticulated jealousy.

Could it be then that what lies at the root of this Christian-Jewish bitterness is a kind of spiritual jealousy? Like the eleven brothers who plotted to murder Joseph the favoured son, and sling his body into a well, have we Gentiles resented, with a murderous resentment, this apparent favouritism? Moltmann in his essay *The Church and Israel* describes the Christian Church as a 'younger sibling in the promissory history of God'.[3] Absolutely. Any parent knows what sibling jealousies can be like.

There are potent seeds of ugly malice here: the Jews, we are told, are the divinely chosen ones, born effortlessly into faith without having to face any of the struggles and agonies of our seemingly lesser Christian commitment. But is it just who they claim to be that galls, or what they *represent*? Is it, more deeply than a question of status, a question of vision and promise and, as the Jews know so well, suffering — and suffering avoided? At the heart of Jewish faith is a hard, ethical and demanding road, the way of the law and the prophets, a way that the Christian church has constantly romanticised, spiritualised and compromised. The Jews, simply by their existence, remind us of it. What is required indeed is 'the painful process of unlearning, and relearning what religion is about'.

What is necessary at the beginning is to attempt to get some grasp on the basics of Jewish faith — the faith of *our* fathers. In what follows I have sketched out in the briefest outline some of the salient features, those basic contours necessary if we are going to take this task of learning to believe again seriously. For this is what must be embarked upon — nothing less than a re-education in faith. It is a matter of the fundamentals — *our* fundamentals as Christians, requiring a willingness to learn again. Rabbi Lionel Blue has written: 'To enter the inner world of the Jewish religion requires an initial stripping, a deliberate unlearning of what religion is about, and a new definition of words.'[4]

However, before we attempt to gain some grasp of these fundamentals, we need to acknowledge that there are other difficulties. Some, looking at the bloodshed and violence, the slaughter of infants, the extermination of other nations — ugly features that are part and parcel of the Old Testament narrative, ask: how is it possible to say yes to a faith that has its roots in such bloody and violent events, events which are characterised as *acts of God*? We need to acknowledge the force of this reaction. Without attempting to explore it in detail, I would make three points. First, the historical period we are dealing with was a bloody and violent one in which small nations preyed mercilessly on each other. A period different, though not perhaps so different, from our own. Second the promise and the vision that the Hebrews were given moved outwards, and ultimately included, in an ethical embrace of justice and peace, *all* nations. Their understandings of God grew from a limited tribal deity to the God of all the earth. Third, the vision was fulfilled and given a new definition of life for all, as we shall see, in the Jew from Nazareth. We need to comprehend their long search from the perspective of its end in him. These points need to be born in mind as we seek to identify the particularly *Jewish* ways of thinking about God and the world.

The Vision

Hebrew religion has its roots in many complex strands of tradition fused together to form one collection of writings which we know as the Old Testament. We shall look briefly at three of these strands. We are concerned here simply to note those distinctive emphases that, above all, express the *character* of Jewish faith.

A good place to begin is with the Abram/Abraham tradition, and specifically the covenant of promise made to him who is the father of the nation in Genesis chapter 15 verses 12 ff. It is a 'showpiece of Old Testament Theology of History',[5] and takes us back to the very beginning — back to the roots. Here is the original promise which was to be their guiding light — the promise of a *land*. To Abram, living in the land of Canaan, God says:

> Know this for certain, that your descendants will be exiles in a land not their own, where they will be slaves and oppressed for four hundred years. But I will pass judgement on the nation that enslaves them and after that they will leave, with many possessions. For your part, you shall go to your fathers in peace; you shall be buried at a ripe old age. In the fourth generation they will come back here . . .

When the sun had set and darkness had fallen, there appeared a smoking furnace and a firebrand that went between the two halves. That day Yahweh made a Covenant with Abram in these terms:
   'To your descendants I give this land,
   from the wadi of Egypt to the Great River . . .'

A second passage which well summarises the Exodus tradition is Deuteronomy 26:5ff, one of the very earliest credal confessions. Here is captured the emphasis upon the action of God in *history* as well as the rich promise of a fertile earth:

My father was a wandering Aramean. He went down into Egypt to find refuge there, few in number; but there he became a nation, great, mighty, and strong. The Egyptians ill-treated us, they gave us no peace and inflicted hard slavery upon us so we called to Yahweh the God of our Fathers. Yahweh heard our voice and saw our misery, our toil and depression; and Yahweh brought us out of Egypt with a mighty hand and out-stretched arm with great terror and with signs and wonders. He brought us here and gave us this land, the land where milk and honey flow.

A third strand — the Sinai/law tradition, contains a condition: God's promise of peace and prosperity depends upon Israel's faithful obedience to *the Law*, given through Moses. In the introduction to the giving of the law at Sinai in Exodus 19.3 we read:

Moses then went up to God, and Yahweh called to him from the mountain, saying, 'Say this to the House of Jacob, declare this to the sons of Israel, You yourselves have seen what I did with the Egyptians, how I carried you on eagle's wings and brought you to myself. From this you know that now, if you obey my voice and hold fast to my covenant, you of all the nations shall be my very own for all the earth is mine.'

It is important to note here that obedience to the law and the covenant is *preceded* by God's loving liberating action: 'I carried you on eagle's wings and brought you to myself.'

God's saving action in history, the promise of a fertile land and obedient living out of the ethical character of this Holy God — three fundamentally Jewish strands. What implications can we draw from these as to how the Jews think about God and the world?

First, we need to grasp that for the Jew, history and time are sacred. They are the means by which God reveals himself — his action is to be discerned in and through them. Second, the promise is not of heavenly reward or blessing but the gift of a land overflowing with fertility and goodness. The hope is therefore materialist and uncompromisingly this worldly. Third, the fulfilment of the promise depended on the living out of the law — the Torah — which was the heart of their life. It is a detailed code that prescribes both worship and social morality and embodies the character of God himself. Fourth, we need to note throughout, the constant sense of forward movement. Faith in the Old Testament is future-orientated. The God of Abraham, the God of the Exodus and the God of the Promise is the God 'with future as his essential nature',[6] the God whose very name — Yahweh — given to Moses when he hears the call to bring the Israelites out (Ex 3) is pregnant with future. It is most accurately translated: 'I will be what I will be', or 'I cause to be what I cause to be' i.e., you will know me through the events that are to come . . . [7] Even when they have entered the land and the promise would seem to have been fulfilled, we find the promise and the vision is itself stretched out, extended, to include at the end of Isaiah, the whole earth. It is as though — like the cloud by day and the fire by night — the promise is itself moving forward, finally to embrace in the embrace of love, justice and peace, the whole creation. Finally we need to appreciate the note of severe monotheism, expressed in the beautiful words of the *Shema* which every faithful Jew will know by heart:

> Hear O Israel:
> The Lord our God is one Lord
> and you shall love the Lord your God with all your
>   heart,
> and with all your soul,
> and with all your might . . . (Deut 6:4ff)

In the Hebrew vision, God is utterly transcendant and fundamentally unknowable so great is his glory. But man is not nothing. In praying, the faithful Jew raises up his hands and blesses God and is blessed by God, it is a reciprocal giving and receiving of blessing. Here there is such a marked contrast from the tone of some strands of Protestant spirituality that repeatedly emphasise human sinfulness and worthlessness. In the Hebrew vision, humans share God's likeness, and are to be stretched by him to our full stature and glory, co-workers with God, co-creators with the Lord, God's partners in the ordering and managing of the earth. The vision is fantastic, beautiful and very demanding: humans full-grown, free, responsible, just, glorious . . . managers *with* God of his good earth.

Idolatry

It is a fantastic vision, yet also severe and demanding. No wonder the Jews struggled with this calling. Who wants that kind of freedom and responsibility with God? Which of us wants to grow up to share that kind of task? It is much easier to be unfree, and construct other lesser gods to worship, easier to cave in to immediate powers and authorities, to cling to our comfortable prejudices, than to respond to the call of the mysterious hidden sovereign God who requires the leaving behind of every other certainty and security and a setting out in search of a promise of justice and peace — Shalom — for the whole earth. Idolatry, the worship of and fixation with lesser more comfortable gods is, in the Hebrew mind, the ultimate sin, for it stops you — dead. It feeds the illusion that you have already got the future in your grasp — that you already *know* the way.

Such idolatry is evident in our society too, in the fixation with those simple political ideologies that are offered as clear-cut solutions to our ills. They appeal to the worst in us and they benefit the rich and powerful and result in dire consequences for the poor. They are idolatrous, and the obsession with them reveals an unwillingness to grow into and discover the image and likeness of the One who is alone sovereign, whose way is always love seeking justice, who is Lord and Lover of *all*, and who will accept no division or diminishment of anything.

This was their vision. But what is their story? We need briefly to outline the sequence of events through which the vision was formed. In this we shall try to get a sense of the way the Hebrews were what we are called to be — a searching people.

The Story

Israel's early story is marked by a constant setting out into the unknown and the paradigm figure of this obedient searching faith is Abraham — *the* exemplar of the meaning of faith. Abraham was a nomadic tribal chieftain living in Mesopotamia when he heard the mysterious call: 'Leave your country, your family and your father's house for the land I will show you' (Gen 12:1). The New Testament author to the Hebrews puts the matter with beautiful simplicity: 'By faith Abraham obeyed the call to set out for a country that was the inheritance given to him and his descendants, and he set out without knowing where he was going' (Heb 11:8). Here is established the distinctive pattern of Hebrew faith — fundamentally *nomadic*. It is a faith that moves, a faith that hopes, a faith that goes in search of a new future, a faith that does not know the shape of that future. . . .

This same fundamental pattern is there in the Exodus which is the foundational event of Jewish life and consciousness. *Elohim* — the primitive name for God —

meets the young shepherd Moses in the wilderness at Mount Horeb, and calls him to lead the people out: 'So come, I send you to Pharaoh to bring the sons of Israel, my people out of Egypt . . .' (Ex 3:10). The leading out is not easy, and is marked by terrible conflict and destruction. Eventually after a bitter struggle the angel of death passes over Egypt and the firstborn in all the houses which are not marked by the blood on the lintel die. 'Go', is the oppressor's anguished cry, and they are on the move — Israel is born — a travelling pilgrim people. The story of crossing the Red Sea and the death of the pursuing Egyptians is familiar. Faith now becomes a search for the path ahead. Food and nourishment are given just enough for each day. At the Mountain of Sinai they are given the Law that particularly reveals God's severe way. It became their'delight' and the heart of their inner life. It was there in the desert — in lonely dependence — that Israel is forged into a community.

After long journeying, under the leadership of Joshua, the River Jordan is crossed and they enter the land promised to them, only to have to fight a bitter campaign against other nations with other gods. However, instead of a band of oppressed slaves they have now been forged into a people with an identity and vision of human glory and partnership with God — and this prevails.

As Israel's faith — fundamentally nomadic in character — enters a long settled period, there is a constant danger of losing the primitive, monotheistic and ethical character of the early days. In the period of the Judges leading to the glory and power of the monarchy, the promise of future blessings seems to have been fulfilled, though in the royal psalms there is already the hint of the purposes of God moving forward again — now promising a wider divine purpose for the whole earth (Ps 2:7–12; 18:44ff; 72:7–8). However a spiritual rot had set in. In the midst of the glory of the monarchy the simple nomadic faith in the God of the Sinai Covenant and the future promise — is lost. Gradually, corruption, division, moral decay and a fundamental disregard for the inner heart of their life, the social morality of the Mosaic Law, lead inexorably to Israel's downfall. Eventually Jerusalem itself is taken. The people are made captive and in shame led away to Babylon.

And so in the tragic event of the Exile Israel's darkest night sets in. The promise of the land is gone. They are broken, enslaved again and in a strange land — how can they sing the Lord's song? There is a haunting beauty in the ballad of the exiles:

> Beside the streams of Babylon we sat and wept at the memory of Zion, leaving our harps hanging on the poplars there.

> For we had been asked to sing to our captors, to entertain those who had carried us off: 'Sing', they said, 'some hymns of Zion.'

> How could we sing one of Yahweh's hymns in a pagan country?

But God cannot desert his beloved. Through second Isaiah once again the note of promise and a new future is heard. Like a mother comforting her lost child, the prophet proclaims: 'Comfort, comfort my people . . .' and tells of a glorious return to Zion. 'When Yahweh brought Zion's captives home, at first it seemed like a dream'(Ps 126:1). And so they return, and the books of Ezra and Nehemiah tell of the rebuilding of Jerusalem.

The Vision extended

But Israel's destiny was never to be for herself alone. Towards the end of the Old Testament, once again the nomadic God of the future is on the move calling his people forward to a new role — not for Israel alone, nor for a specific land, but this time for the whole earth. What we see towards the end of Isaiah is the extraordinary development and reflowering of hope and purpose for Israel. He is the prophet who has been called 'the originator of a theology of world history'.[8] Seeing the whole course of history as under the control of God, the prophet takes hold of and stretches out the promise to encompass the whole inhabited earth:

> 'I am coming to gather the nations of every language. They shall come to witness my glory. I will give them a sign and send some of their survivors to the nations: to Tarshish, Put, Lud, Mosech, Rosh, Tubal, and Javan, to the distant islands that have never heard of me or seen my glory. They will proclaim my glory to the nations.'
> (Is 66:18,19)

Claus Westermann in his study of *Isaiah 40–66* comments:

> One is amazed at it: here, just as the Old Testament is coming to its end, God's way is already seen as leading from the narrow confines of the chosen people out into the wide, whole world. The annihilation of all the other nations in a great world judgement — no, this is not the final word. But equally, it is not that they all journey to Zion and are absorbed into the community there. The final thing is the way taken by the word, borne by the messengers of his glory, to the peoples who are not Israel, all the nations in the world.[9]

Here we reach the high point of the Jewish search as we know it through the Old Testament, a climactic moment arrived at only after a long trek, in which the understandings of God and his promise had themselves developed, evolved, grown.

As we look back through Israel's history what we can see is an extraordinary and tenacious clinging to, and following of, the God of promise, and a stretching out of the promise, until it embraced the whole world. The original promise to Abraham — that in him all the families of the earth will be blessed (Gen 12:3) — was not forgotten but pursued and worked out, clung to and developed through the whole span of Hebrew history.

What I have been concerned to point out is the distinctively Jewish way of thinking about God, over against so much later thinking in the Christian tradition depicting God as timeless, detached, ethereal and remote. We must try to grasp it, for it was the way that Jesus grew up into. These stories were constantly told and retold, acted out in worship, in home, synagogue and temple, and provided the foundation events of his thinking and praying and believing. At the risk of over-simplification let us summarise. First, it is a sense of a people under God and *with* God constantly moving forward, stepping over boundaries 'a people of tents rather than a temple',[10] with their God as a 'wayfaring God' — bearing in his heart a salvation purpose in history and for history. Second, it is a sense of God promising not spiritual other worldly comfort, or 'timeless truths'— those things which have become the stock-in-trade of most clergy and religious leaders — but land, bread, water, milk and honey, vines, figs, pomegranates . . . material necessities and delights savoured and blessed. Third, it is a sense of a God who insists on justice and burns with compassion and love for the poor, the widow, the orphan, the stranger and the alien. It is this sense — this uniquely Jewish sense clung to despite appalling setbacks — of an historical, materialist, compassionate, holy God of justice, moving forward and leading history towards his purpose of universal salvation for *all*, that grasped the Hebrew heart, inspired the Hebrew search, and is the gift of the Hebrew hope for all humankind.

Betrayal

We have dwelt on the vision. But it was not of course one continuing faith success story. The Jews were human too. There were constant betrayals, persistent idolatry, and despairing, persecuted and isolated prophets. Perhaps the most vivid picture is of Elijah fleeing into the desert having heard that Ahab had killed all the prophets of Israel. There he sits, despairing, under a furze bush and wishes he were dead. 'Yahweh,' he said, 'I have had enough. Take my life' (1 Kings 19:4). The prophets are those who hold fast to the ancient vision, with its emphasis on justice and righteousness, interpreting it afresh in each generation. Through them over and over again, God is pictured as exasperated and deeply wounded by the faithlessness of his people and their blatant disregard for the poor and he brings harsh judgement — it is a dominant note of the eighth century prophets. God is portrayed as insulted and enraged by the behaviour of Israel and the way the poor are being systematically robbed and trampled on. Jeremiah and Hosea — prophets of God in whose line Jesus saw himself — make quite explicit that to do justice is to know God:

> Did not your father eat and drink and do justice and righteousness? Then it was well with him. He judged the cause of the poor and needy; then it was well. *Is not this to know me* says the Lord (Jer 22:15,16).

And from Hosea:

> Sons of Israel, listen to the words of Yahweh, for Yahweh indites the inhabitants of the country: there is no fidelity, no tenderness no knowledge of God in the country, only perjury and lies, slaughter, theft, adultery and violence, murder after murder (Hos 4:1–2).

The people are warned repeatedly that God will bring devastating judgement. But always deeper than his anger is his love: the God who has loved Israel with an intimate, even sexual love, cannot abandon her (Ezek 16). Always, even in the darkest time there is the promise ahead of a new beginning and a new hope.

Somehow the Church too, built on the foundation stories of Jesus and the Old Testament has abandoned, or just drifted away from these distinctive understandings. There has been a fundamental parting of the ways and the implications of these understandings is still largely lost upon us.

First, history. If the God of the Hebrews is the God who acts in history and promises future blessing in history — for Israel and ultimately a universal hope for the whole earth, then the clear implication is that still he is the One whose purposes need to be discerned and looked for in the complexities and struggles of public and political affairs. The Hebrew God is a political God. There is no getting away from this. There is plenty of room for discussion as to what this means and we need to be wary of naive and simplistic conclusions, but to deny it as is constantly done, is to deny the fundamental nature of the Hebrew hope.

Second, the material world. If the promise was for a land — the earth and the good things of that good earth, and if the Hebrews were not moved by a vision of some kind of merely 'spiritual' comfort, no more will people be today. Like poor people everywhere they knew that what they needed were the basic things of the earth for their survival, fulfilment and celebration, and they were drawn by the very specific promise of these . . . land, work, jobs, food, shelter . . . and wine 'to make glad the heart of man' (Ps 104:15).

Third, justice and social morality. The inner heart of Hebrew faith, that which gave them their distinctive identity, was their love of and adherence to the law. In the books of the law, we see a detailed framework of mutual obligation — interdependence — which guarded the poor and the weak, made a place for the stranger and the alien, ensured a sharing of resources, and nurtured that sense of being a people — a community — together. It is almost impossible for us to grasp the meaning of this; the Hebrew concept of personality is a corporate one. Our notion of separate individuality would have been entirely foreign to them.

It is these themes above all that are dominant in the Hebrew story, and it is these themes that the churches must seek to recover at every level of their life.

Go into any comfortable church in comfortable Britain. What do you hear? What has happened to this faith? Instead of any attempt to wrestle or engage with this demanding vision and hope, what is constantly on offer is a weak brew of personal private comfort in a nasty hostile world. What seems to be lacking so often is any sense of searching for the divine promise and purpose in our history, our society and our politics. Where is our promised future in history built on justice with material blessing for all? Somehow Christian thought has surrendered this. It has reduced, watered down and reformulated Christian hope in almost totally other-worldly terms. It has been an extraordinary denial of our ancestry. Perhaps we are slowly discovering that a religion that cannot provide change and hope and new life in and for this world has itself died; and has about it that strange dead smell that you find in crematoria, a religion of plastic flowers, clean well-scrubbed buildings and a strong emphasis on order and submission. Such religion can do nothing to challenge current idolatries. Perhaps we need Paul's rebuke to the Corinthians again but turned on its head. If our hope in Christ is for the other world only, we are the most unfortunate of all people. And if this is the tone and shape of our religion there are dangers too, for in the absence of the emphasis upon the search for God's purposes *now*, inevitably a vacuum is created and we look for it through other means: religions of personal therapy and self-fulfilment thrive, or various brands of fundamentalism. Both these strands may be important in the personal growth of Christians as we shall see in Part Two, but they are strands that are fundamentally insubstantial in the face of the Hebrew vision, spelled out in the law and the prophets. We may try to avoid it, as the Hebrews did, but this remains our vision too. Perhaps it is comforting that they also ran from this hope. The Old Testament pictures God's people as repeatedly in flight into the worship of, and easy commitment, to the surrounding gods of the nations. They ran away from the demanding vision of their own prophets whom they persecuted. And yet they were turned back — back to the hard road of God's promise — which is the way of hope for us all. So we are led to the question in our society: What is God asking of us now in his project of building a righteous society of justice and peace? In Part Three we shall look at this more closely.

As we have looked at their vision, perhaps we can be clearer now why we have persecuted the Jews. They are

our forefathers — members of our faith family — and by
their very existence they remind us of God's project, God's
calling of us to seek his Kingdom, and his demand of love
that we be co-builders with him of that Kingdom here 'on
earth as in heaven'.

A restless longing

Christians claim that Jesus the Jew fulfilled the Jewish
hope and opened up that hope for all. He was not just part
of the promise — he *was* the promise. We shall look at that
in the next chapter. But before we do we need to set
the scene for his announcement of the Kingdom. What
happened in the actual progress of events? We need to
complete the Jewish story up to his coming. Towards the
end of the Old Testament period, the clouds over Israel
gather and the nation descends into a dark and bitter
period.

> After 63 BC the situation of the Jews in Palestine was a
> particularly bitter one. They had returned from their
> captivity in Babylon exulting in God as king who had
> again delivered them. They had then known almost two
> centuries of virtual independence only to fall prey again
> to Egyptians and Syrians. Under Judas Maccabee and
> his successors they had known another century of inde-
> pendence, and even a restoration of their state to some-
> thing of its ancient glory. But now their situation was
> worse than ever. The Romans ruled in the land, and
> Jewish High Priests, the representatives of God to the
> people and of the people before God, were appointed by
> Roman fiat. After 6 AD the situation worsened, for at
> that time the Romans began to rule Jerusalem directly
> by means of a Roman procurator.

> Under these circumstances the Jewish people continued
> to evoke the ancient myth, but now the formulations
> have a note of intensity about them, a note almost of
> despairing hope.[11]

Israel now clings tenaciously to her faith in the God of history and justice: there is born in the people a desperate restless searching and longing for the Kingdom to come. The Essenes retreat to the caves of Judea and wait for the Messiah and the defeat of the 'sons of darkness'; apocalyptic writings appear with visions of cosmic battles and the eventual triumph of good over evil; the Zealots take to the hills ready to fight for him who will come and redeem Israel; in the synagogues the longing for the Kingdom — the reign of the God of history, material blessing and justice for the poor, is expressed in the Kaddish prayer which was in regular use immediately before the time of Jesus:

> Magnified and sanctified be his great name in the world that he has created according to his will.
> May he establish his Kingdom in your lifetime and in your days and in the lifetime of all the house of Israel, even speedily and at a near time.[12]

This agonised restless longing was the background both to Jesus's prayer — 'your Kingdom come on earth' — and Jesus's proclamation 'the Kingdom of God *is* close at hand.'

It is a restlessness and longing experienced today in our society severed as it is from any living religious tradition. As the ideology of 'possessive individualism' gets its hold in all of us fuelling anxiety and breeding division and bitterness the question is: where can we find the vision, the hope and the spiritual impulse that may release people from the tyranny of individual greed, enabling us to belong together — so we really know what *Shalom* means? This is a cry felt throughout both Church and community. The Jews have more than some clues. Of course we cannot translate the situation of ancient Israel into our situation. We are not a nation in a special covenant relationship with God. We are a highly complex multi-racial pluralist society at the end of the twentieth century. But nevertheless, the Jews offer us a vision of the human community under God which is both daunting and compelling, and which must encourage us to resist those lesser understandings of God — the god of static moral ideals; the god of timeless and abstract truths; the god of spiritual comfort and heavenly reward for the individual soul — that lack their dynamic element. The God who we both need and fear is the Holy One of Israel who requires justice, has a yearning love for the poor and brokenhearted, and is to be searched for in and through our bloodied history. He is the God who promises in his Kingdom the things of the earth as his gift. He is the God of *Shalom*, which means the place where everyone and everything belongs.

As we reflect on this inheritance of Jesus the Jew who is for us Christians both brother and Lord, there is the question: *How did Jesus fulfil this search and is he the way by which we Christians can come home to our Jewish home, as well as being the One who sends us out on a renewed search for that Kingdom?* To that second story we must now turn.

Chapter 2: The Heart of the Search

In this first part we are in search of some basic understandings. What is meant by the Kingdom of God? The actual phrase itself occurs very little in the Old Testament though it comes to the fore in the restless, searching and barren period leading up to the coming of Jesus. From the midst of the cry of the people articulated in the Kaddish prayer: 'May he establish his Kingdom in your lifetime . . .' Jesus picked it out and made it the centrepiece of his message: 'The time *has* come, and the Kingdom of God is close at hand. Repent, and believe the good news' (Mark 1:15). The good news is that the longed-for Kingdom is now dawning — at long last *the* moment has arrived. As we saw in the previous chapter, time for the Jew was fundamental in God's purposes. It is in time and through the process of time and history that God acts. 'Now', says this Jesus, 'the time has arrived . . .'.

If we are to understand *what* he said and did, we cannot take Jesus' message — which is for all time — out of the particular time in which he proclaimed it: first century Palestine. The search for the Kingdom of God in the preaching of Jesus requires some preliminary attention to the social context of that preaching.

The Social Context

The Palestinian world of Jesus's time was no calm sea of untroubled tranquillity, but a seething turbulent ferment of factional division, of fervent longing and the loss of any unifying vision of the Jewish hope. While the leadership of the Jewish community struggled under the Roman presence and was bitterly divided amongst themselves, the ordinary common people particularly outside Jerusalem —

in Galilee where Jesus came from — suffered under the weight of Roman taxation. They felt alienated and disowned by their own religious leaders, and cut off from God's promises which in the past had been their lifeblood — and which they had thought was their birthright. As the poor suffered, four principal religious/political groupings vied with one another in competing understandings of God's purposes for Israel.[1] We shall look at their different strategies for the survival of the nation in the face of the Roman occupation and how they interpreted God's promises for his people.

First there were the *Pharisees*. The name itself literally means those 'separated off' from the common people. Their strategy for the survival of Jewish identity in the face of the pagan Roman presence was vigorously to assert their Jewishness by obsessive attention to the detailed minutiae of the law of Moses, and by their claim taught in the synagogues that God's favour was only to be gained by the most rigorous adherence to that law. Not content with the primitive Mosaic tradition, the Pharisees over the years had developed a further set of prescriptions and prohibitions and interpretations for every tiny detail of daily life. In effect they 'built a wall around the law' and demanded obedience to a twofold law. Their influence in Israel was very widespread as their life was centred on the synagogues, and in terms of hope, their focus had moved away from the this-worldly tradition of the Mosaic hope, to the resurrection of the dead and the hope of eternal life — for those who kept the law as they saw it.

The *Sadducees* from whom the Chief Priests came, tended to be drawn from the old aristocratic and conservative Jewish families. They had a similar high regard for the primitive Mosaic law though they resisted the further detailed interpretations and prescriptions of the Pharisees, and had no time for their belief in the resurrection of the dead. As they saw it, they remained loyal to the ancient this-worldly hope for a promised land comprising a religious nation state centred on the Temple in Jerusalem, and so their approach to the Romans could be summed up as resentful pragmatism: they were willing to collaborate in order to ensure the continuation of the temple worship, not least because their 'privileged economic position depended on the Temple tax'.[2]

The *Zealots* (i.e. 'the fervent or fanatic ones')[3] were the freedom-fighters of Jesus' time. Nearer to the common people, they were particularly strong in the country regions like Galilee away from Jerusalem, where wild talk was of a political Messiah who would be sent by God to lead them in their armed struggle. It seems clear that at least some among Jesus's close group were either Zealots themselves or those very sympathetic to Zealot thinking.

Finally, there were the *Essenes* from whom John the Baptiser may well have come. The most famous Essene community was the community of Qumran, the library of which was discovered in 1947. While most Essene communities were founded in the desert, it is suggested that Essenes also lived in Palestinian cities. Their strategy was total withdrawal from the world into men-only communities where they led an austere life of continuous study of the scriptures, daily ritual washing, and the sharing of goods, while they waited for the coming of the Messiah and the 'victory of the sons of light over the sons of darkness'.[4]

Under their shared oppression these groupings competed with one another in their claim to be the holy remnant of Israel. They hated the Romans but they also hated every Israelite who did not belong to their particular group. In this atmosphere of sectarian suspicion and division, the majority of Palestinian Jews were too poor to be politically or religiously active. In response to the demands of the dominant groups, the Pharisees and the Sadducees, they would have been quite unable to observe the detailed minutiae of the law upon which salvation depended. The law, which had been in the psalms of David — 'sweeter than honey to my mouth, and a light on my path' (Ps 119:103, 105) — now had become a crushing guilt-inducing burden shutting out the vast majority from the blessings of the covenant. In this situation, special contempt was reserved by the religious leaders for those whose life was seen to be clearly sinful — deviant from the will of Yahweh: tax gatherers who collaborated actively with the hated Romans, thieves, brigands, prostitutes.

A New World

It is against this background that Jesus comes into Galilee seizing the moment: 'The time *has* come . . .' It was an extraordinary message of a radically new world of joy and abundance breaking into the midst of this present world. It was open to all although only entered into if you turn your back on every attitude and assumption that currently dominates your life. In the self-righteous posturings of these religious groupings, mental worlds had shrunk and shrivelled into small hardened mutually hostile divisions which excluded the common people and condemned the sinful. Jesus came insisting on something utterly new — a root and branch reversal of *all* existing modes of thought. The reality that gripped him was the cherishing, valuing, accepting and totally all-embracing love of God for every single creature and person no matter what they had done or were. A love only to be received as pure gift — without merit or effort.

What we need to grasp is that Jesus was not just bringing a more refined or deeper teaching. What he announced was potentially the *end of the world* as we know it and the beginning of a new world, but one which we can scarcely glimpse as we are so enmeshed in the attitudes and actions of the old one. In his particular social context, his words and actions immediately and inevitably met with fierce opposition. To the Pharisees this proclamation of the Kingdom amounted to a demolition job on the detailed systems of religious practice that were their proud boast. It cut at the root of the sense of privilege and class that sustained the Sadducee. It showed up as narrow, absurd and unnecessary the obsessive practices of the Essene. And it was capable of melting and transforming the hard militant heart of the Zealot. Above all it opened up life chances for the ordinary common people who the Gospel tells us flock to him in their thousands, and it reached into the hardest and most disturbed hearts of humans degraded in corruption. To the Pharisees he is reported as saying: 'The prostitutes and the tax gatherers go into the Kingdom of God ahead of you!' (Matt 21:31). Small wonder that very rapidly we read of them plotting to destroy him. The effect of his preaching and action was to them utterly scandalous — destroying what was left of Jewish substance and identity, and he *had* to be stopped. When men feel their identity and religion threatened — they become very vicious.

Right from the outset Jesus of Nazareth in his faithfulness to the Kingdom was on an inevitable collision course with all the dominant groups. This new in-breaking Reign of God stood in radical contradistinction to every earthly rule and justification. It was not a question of 'bias to the poor', it was *only* the poor, those who knew their need, who could enter and enjoy it. The rich, secure in their own systems, would inevitably be sent away empty. Hence their fury. Hence crucifixion.

However, before we get into the detail of our quest, we need to say something about the approach to be adopted. The purpose of this chapter is to focus very briefly on Jesus of Nazareth and his proclamation of the coming Reign of God. What did he understand by the Kingdom? To those unfamiliar with New Testament studies it is important to grasp that the announcement of this Kingdom, now dawning in his person, was the focus of Jesus's life. He was grasped by the conviction that God was doing a new thing — no less than the final thing — in and through him.

Looking at the Gospels, and particularly Paul's letters which are the earliest documents in the New Testament, it is clear that the focus has shifted from the Kingdom to Jesus himself, now proclaimed as 'the Christ'. He became the focus of faith, indeed he had become the Kingdom. So the centre of Paul's preaching is not the Kingdom of God, but Jesus Christ crucified and risen, now ascended and Lord of all. It was to proclaim faith in Jesus as Lord and Christ that the whole New Testament was written by men and women in early communities of faith to share and bring that faith to their world:

> What we have seen and heard we are telling you so that you too may be in union with us, as we are in union with the Father and with his Son Jesus Christ (1 John 1:3).

In this 'search for the Kingdom' we are looking back to the stage prior to faith in Christ, to the earlier stage of asking the question as honestly as we can, who was Jesus of Nazareth and what was the Kingdom which he proclaimed into a fearful and desperate world? That earlier stage is embedded in the Gospels and it is possible to see the outline of this historical figure in the midst of the sometimes ornate faith embellishments of the early church, and even hear his words themselves, what Jeremias has called the *ipsissima vox* — the voice itself.[5]

In other words, we are not beginning with Jesus the saviour, pre-existent before time, born of a virgin mother, who went about doing good and healing and performing miracles, was crucified, dead and buried, and then raised on the third day and is now ascended and Lord and will come again at the end of time. This is the creed. This is the faith tradition of the Church — a faith tradition nourished and developed in worship and adoration, like a painter colouring in, touching up, and adding to, a fundamentally simple picture. It is a faith tradition which grew and developed in the early communities of faith — before finally it was written down in the letters and the Gospels. They were written from faith to evoke faith but at the heart of this faith tradition stands an historical person: Jesus the man from Nazareth who proclaimed his conviction in the coming Reign of God, and lived out that Reign even to death. That is the focus of this search for basic understandings. Where do we begin?

Our question is, what is this Kingdom message? First it may be helpful to state what it was not. Jesus of Nazareth was not the founder of one more school of religious teaching — indeed there is no evidence that he set out to found any new religion (and to that extent the title of one of the best known works on the historical Jesus: *The Founder of Christianity*[6] is somewhat misleading). He was not a teacher of religious 'doctrine' as such at all, nor was he interested in the moral 'improvement' of his disciples or his society. He was struggling to convey something altogether more demanding and absolute, more other-worldly and yet totally to do with this world. By a variety of artful words and actions, using particularly the practice of storytelling, meal giving, prayer, signs of healing and ultimately his own life, he sought to open up to the men and women around him something that was immediately available — 'in the midst of them' — which would entirely transform their lives: nothing less than the end of this world and the beginning of a new one. But they were too blind, stubborn and proud to see and embrace it. This something above all was very good news! But to embrace it meant abandoning all previous ways of thinking and behaving. How could he get people to *see*?

Parables

The first and pre-eminent device he used was the story – the parables of the Kingdom. Whole libraries have been written on Jesus' use of the parable, and what is presented here is a brief survey of some of them. While there is a lot to be said for detailed study of the parable tradition, at another level it is all remarkably simple only requiring imagination and the ability to enter unreservedly into the heart of the story.

The main thing to grasp is that these parables are ordinary stories that reach into the most everyday, ordinary, commonplace world of people's daily lives. We are taken into the kitchen where dough is rising on the housewife's table; into the sitting room where a woman has lost a coin and is frantically searching under all the furniture; out on to the fell side where a shepherd has left his whole flock and gone on to search for one lost sheep; into the market place where men are hanging around waiting for work; into the fields where a farmer is scattering corn seed. Next there is the situation of a family where a son has gone missing and then suddenly turns up, and to the fury of the hard-working elder brother there is a riotous party. And so it goes on . . . parties, bread, coins, sheep, seeds, family turmoil. Commonplace everyday situations and characters of a first century agricultural world.

As with all stories that really touch and mirror ordinary life the whole attention is caught up. These are things people understood. This was their world. They knew what it was like to lose valuable coins. They knew what it was like to run the risk of the lonely Jerusalem to Jericho road. They had seen the Priest and the Levite in their long robes scuttling by on their priestly business. They had narrowed their eyes at the approach of a hated Samaritan. They had slunk into the back of the temple and heard and glimpsed beneath lowered eyelids the praying of the proud Pharisees. They had seen the birds hungrily gobble seed at the edge of the corn field. They knew the bleating of lost sheep in the high hills. They have sweated in the heat of the sun for casual earnings. They knew what it was like to be in debt. They have seen the birds nest in the branches of the mustard tree, the corn sprout in spring, the dough rise, they have also heard lavish stories of the banquets of the rich. These stories reach into the detailed fabric of their lives.

But, these are not just heart-warming stories that have a bracing moral bite: with Jesus' stories, there is always an explosive shock effect, what the Roman Catholic scholar Schillebeeckx has called 'a scandalising centre'[7] that blasts apart conventional ways of thinking revealing the open secret of the joyful Reign of God.

It is beyond the scope here to attempt to examine each and every one of the parables. What we are engaged in is a search, and the parables offer us clues that help us on the way to discovering what is at the heart of this Kingdom. Here, as in the whole of this chapter, I am much indebted to the approach and sequence of thought in James P. Mackey's book: *Jesus the Man and the Myth*[8] and in particular his superb chapter 'The life of Jesus' and I have followed that sequence here. I know of nowhere where it has been said more sharply and clearly. Mackey divides the parables into five stages, each collection of parables taking us nearer to the secret of the Kingdom message.

The first clue comes in the group of parables which we may call: 'The joyful discovery of things hidden or lost.' The woman who lost a coin and swept through the house until she found it and then ran and rejoicing told all her neighbours (Luke 15:8); the shepherd who left the flock and went up into the hills to find the one lost sheep and returned rejoicing with it across his shoulders (Luke 15.4); the precious pearl (Matt 15:45); the treasure lying buried in the field (Matt 15:44). It is not easy for us in our urban modern culture to get inside the narrative of these stories particularly as they are already deadened by familiarity but the attempt must be made. Try to embed yourself in the detail as Jesus tells it. Remember something you have lost, something which really matters. You have searched high and low in every nook and cranny, under every chair and bed, on every windowsill and behind every bookshelf in your house. Where is it? You are beside yourself with the need to find this object. Then suddenly something is moved and there it is. What do you feel? Enormous relief and joy coupled with a fresh delight in the thing that was lost which perhaps previously you had taken entirely for granted. You want to rush and tell others and share the joy. Suddenly this thing is enormously valuable to you and you swear you will take enormous care of it and never ever lose it again!

Next are the parables that emphasise the need to be both ready and waiting (the ten bridesmaids, Matt 25:1), and quick and decisive (the unjust steward, Luke 16:1) in response to this Kingdom. The clue here is the need to grasp the moment when it comes — to take risks — and not to be found messing about with other concerns so that you miss the moment being offered, or are simply too concerned or afraid to see it. The parable of the great feast or what could be called the parable of the 'over-busy self-obsessed invitees' particularly resonates with us. A banquet is prepared and the table is groaning with good things. Come and eat and belong and rejoice says the host. Apologies start flooding in: thanks for the invitation but I'm into real estate so I'm afraid I am just too busy; I've just bought some new farm equipment (five yoke of oxen denotes a rich farmer) — frightfully sorry; you'll understand if I tell you that I've just got married — so naturally we won't be able to come. Busy, successful, attractive and above all private people structuring their own comfortable private worlds — too busy for the feast, for the banquet of the Kingdom. So it is those living on the streets, who have no plans, no diaries, no schedules, no private comforts, who fill the house until it bursts.

According to this Jesus then, something is on offer here that will awaken a new joy, and will open up new contacts with friends and neighbours and strangers making us rich. But it will require decisiveness and a willingness to take risks and cross new thresholds abandoning business and opting into community with strangers and poor people. But there is a note of warning: the opportunity can come very suddenly, and unless we look out for it we may well miss it.

There is a different kind of warning in a third group of parables. We are told the story of a king who goes to war (Luke 14:31) and has to give up half way because he knows he has not enough resources to finish the job. These are people who set out on a quest without reckoning on the cost. The story seems to suggest that this something will cost a lot and there may be fierce opposition. We are reminded again of the parable of the treasure buried in the field; buying the field didn't just make deep inroads into his bank balance — it cost the treasure seeker every single thing he had. Unless we realise this, says Jesus, it might be better not to set out on the quest at all.

Fourthly, there are parables that give a clearer idea of the nature of this cost for they are stories which are profoundly offensive. If we are to be citizens of this Kingdom then we had better realise we shall fundamentally offend basic concepts of right and wrong, of justice and reward and punishment that for many are the very foundation stones of social morality. Amongst these which we may call 'parables of joy and offence', are: the Prodigal Son (Luke 15:11); labourers in the vineyard (Matt 20:1); the Pharisee and the tax collector (Luke 18:9); the good Samaritan (Luke 10:29). Each mercilessly strikes at the roots of cherished assumptions about both Jewish faith and traditions, but more generally at how things simply *ought to be* in any righteous and right-thinking person's world. Jesus says the Kingdom of God is like a father who when his son had gone off abroad spending half of his whole fortune on a life of excess, and then is reduced to looking after pigs on a Gentile farm — even eating the pigs' food (and remember what that would have meant to a pious Jew) — and then out of desperation decided to return home with a rehearsed speech of profound contrition in his pocket, was welcomed back with tears of joy by the waiting father without so much as a moment to listen to any apology. To the upright Jewish audience this is appalling. The boy had behaved by any standards abominably: he had wasted money; he had overstepped every single one of the commandments; he had deserted the family home taking a large slice of the property, had got through the whole lot dragging the family name into the dirt and had ended up working for a Gentile farmer eating pig food. He deserved to be severely rebuked and thoroughly punished. To suggest that the Kingdom of God is about him being given a splendid party wearing again the best clothes of his father and the family ring on his finger . . . it is very profoundly offensive. Jesus has gone too far. The fuming rage of the Pharisee is mirrored in the older brother's indignation as he comes in from the field at the end of yet another hard long day working on the family farm, to hear there is a party for this rake.

Then there is the story of the labourers who waited for work (Matt 20:1). The first was hired in the early morning and worked through the heat of the day tending the vines and doing the back-breaking work of carrying the fruit to the farm all for a promised wage at the end of the day. As they queue to be paid they discover that the men who were hired in the last hour as the pace of work slackened and the sun went down are treated in exactly the same way — and get the same wage! Again it is outrageous offending basic concepts of fairness. In the story of the Pharisee and the publican (Luke 18:10), it is easy here to miss the point and see the Pharisee as a pious prig. In fact he is simply repeating what is true: he has kept the law; he has paid the tithe (a tenth of all he possesses — no small offering); he prays regularly at the appointed hour; he has faithfully kept the commandments. All in all, genuinely a pillar of society — a thoroughly moral and righteous person. The tax collector by contrast has been pocketing taxes and aiding the Romans in the oppression of the Jews and has failed to observe one iota of recognised religious practice. Yet it is he, and not the Pharisee, says this Jesus, who is the one who is justified and goes home righteous in the sight of God. Finally the story of 'the Priest and the Levite passing by' (Luke 10:29ff) — or good Samaritan. It is hard for us again to appreciate the effect in this story. Jesus tells an everyday occurrence of mugging on the road from Jerusalem to Jericho. The two who pass by, no doubt about their spiritual business, are the defenders of Jewish orthodoxy. In their busy lives as teachers and leaders of the community they cannot be concerned with the time-wasting dirty business of helping some poor wretch in the ditch. Besides it would be dangerous and risky and they too might be mugged. All very understandable. By contrast it is a hated Samaritan who binds up the wounds of the victim, puts him on the donkey, takes him to the inn, stays the night, and offers to pay yet more to the innkeeper when he returns if more is needed. Note the excess of generous giving that characterises the behaviour of the Samaritan.

Joy, decision, cost, offence. Lastly Mackey points us to a group of parables that are full of hope and power conveying the sense that from small beginnings there is something unstoppable here which will ultimately triumph despite all appearances to the contrary. Think, said Jesus, of the

bubbling, fermenting power of yeast penetrating and rais-
ing heavy flattened dough (Matt 13:33); think of the tiny
mustard seed which over time grows into a great tree with
spreading branches where the birds of the air nest (Matt
13:31); think of the farmer who sows his seed in the sure
confidence that — without worry — the harvest *will* come
(Mark 4:26). A small hidden power which will, if allowed,
transform everything that it touches.

What is it? 'What is the pattern of experience which the
evocative power of the imagery evokes at the very deepest
level it can reach?'[9] What is it that brings to birth in us
the most delighted joy and comes always somehow new?
What is it that may demand high risk and rapid action to
secure it? What is it that if we are to remain true to it may
bring upon us opposition and scorn and could even cost
us our very lives? What is it that is lost to us when we are
busily obsessed with our own self-importance? What is it
that requires a certain emptiness, openness, abandoning
diaries and schedules? What is it that will upset and offend
the most prized values of both his and our society, values
that say that the good things of life only should belong
to those who have earned and worked for them — that
fundamentally we are only what we make ourselves to be?
What is it that is deeper than these particular assumptions — at root atheistic — believing as they do there is
no life beyond that which we can earn in the market place?
What perception is it, that if sufficiently believed and
waited on has the power to transform disparate scattered
people into communities of celebration and joyfulness and
healing as surely as yeast creates out of dull flat dough —
bread, the very staff of life? It is the perception that life
itself, is pure gift. Gift to be received and rejoiced in, to be
shared and extended to all people no matter who they are
or what they have done. 'To discover or to rediscover life
and existence, all life and all existence, as the most precious
thing we know, always already there and offered for our
acceptance, is to see life as a gift to us or, in the original
meaning of the word, as grace.'[10] If we are able to see all
life, ourselves, and all existence in these terms, and stop

trying to earn and justify that which is already totally given, then we shall arrive in what Jesus called the Kingdom of God — the arena where we celebrate the gift of life, are enabled to give to others, and in holding to this truth are prepared to give up life itself for the sake of this truth, which is paradoxically greater than life.

It is surely right to insist that it is this which is at the heart of Jesus's stories, the cause of both the most profound joy, furious offence, and in the end crucifixion. Such a radical reversal of life's deepest perceptions meant inevitably that it was the poor, those who knew they had nothing to offer but their need and hurt who entered first, who were able to receive the gift. 'Happy are you poor, yours is the Kingdom of heaven' (Matt 5:1). The rich were to be seen either hesitating as in the sad story of the rich young ruler, or creeping to him by night as Nicodemus did, or otherwise indignantly tearing their robes in fury and shouting, away with this man.

Parable then is the tool reaching into the depths of ordinary life to shock and awaken the listener satiated, deadened and cut off by religion into the startling recognition that life is abundant gift — as children who are natural inhabitors of the Kingdom already know — and the world when seen like that is changed.

Meals

If the parables were the scandalising device to open up and make possible perceptions of the Kingdom, that by the shock of the story people might see, Jesus' habit which is clearly grounded in the very earliest strata of the tradition of eating regularly with sinners and tax collectors and the riff-raff of his day was the most vivid enactment of the life of that Kingdom. 'This man,' they said, 'welcomes sinners and eats with them' (Luke 15:2).

What can we learn from these meals about the life of the Kingdom? To try to grasp the full significance of what these meals mean we need to reflect firstly and briefly on the scandal of this activity in the particular social and religious context of the time; and secondly reflect on our own experience of meals in our own very different age. Firstly, from the taunt of Matthew 11:19, 'look a glutton and a drunkard, friend of tax collectors and sinners . . .' we can glean that they were undoubtedly joyful, lengthy and festive occasions! We may assume that the drinking, eating, singing and dancing went on late. Jeremias adds the useful hint too that the word used in Mark 2:15 for 'recline' at the table (*katakeisthai*) signified a festive meal — 'for ordinary meals people sat at table'.[11]

Secondly, as with the stories there was offence. Meals are an altogether more slapdash affair in our own culture but in his time to eat in someone's house at table was an honour. 'It was an offer of peace, trust, brotherhood and forgiveness; in short, sharing at table meant sharing life.'[12] Here was Jesus offering life to all comers, celebrating life as gift, not piously or in a spirit of righteous concern for those poor people, but loving it — 'a glutton and a drunkard' he was called — the *friend* of tax collectors and sinners. He knows life is gift from God. Celebration is the most appropriate mode of being human. In his presence they are learning that too. They are brought from out of the cold darkness of exclusion into the warm acceptance of belonging. And it is all gift. To the proud Pharisee watching from the doorway the whole thing is disgustingly offensive. By the action of this Rabbi, sacred religious practice is dishonoured, and the social order is potentially threatened.

To get to the heart of this activity of Jesus as a meal-giver, Mackey encourages us to reflect deeply on our own experience of the meal. Ask yourself what does a meal at its best mean? What is expressed? What is happening? Think of meals in your family and amongst friends. When we gather together round the table to receive and be sustained by food and share in this experience, we are at root entering into a gift relationship. We do not come to the table like hungry pigs to a trough, or at least even if many households seem like that — and ours is no exception! — this is not how the meal should really be. In this experience as much as any other, we are offering one another the gift of life. Of course a lot of work on our part has gone into it: the land has to be dug, the seed sown, the crops raised and gathered in, the corn milled, the fire or oven made ready, the table laid and prepared, the bread baked — and brought to the table. Human hands and ingenuity have puzzled and worked and sweated to make it. But acknowledging and celebrating all this, the deeper truth is that it is given. And this is what the liturgy of the Eucharist says — a liturgy of production:

> 'Blessed are you O lord our God King of the Universe
> For by your goodness we have this bread to offer which
> earth has given and human hands have made . . .'

We sit, or recline at table and in the circle of our particular community or family. We wait until all are present. We are together — ready. The place is prepared, the table decorated. We acknowledge the gift of one another in silence or words. And then we receive the gift of life and offer to our neighbours that gift and share together in mutual giving and receiving of that which is all gift. 'Every meal fulfils the basic biological need, but it also advertises and realises the fact of life that at a deeper level life depends on our being together, serving each other and sharing, not like animals who happen to converge on the same morsels of food to fight over them . . . it makes real, brings us into contact with those experiences and realities in which life is maintained and enhanced, not just with the physical food but with the fellowship sitting together in peace and harmony, serving each other and sharing the good things provided.' Mackey goes on: '. . . No other ritual could half as effectively convey to human beings the experience of God as the author of life.'[13] This is the meal at its best, and most families and communities glimpse it, even if in our striving, earn-life-for-yourself culture, communities are split up, families have been shrunk and divided, and the meal has become an instant packaged thing 'consumed' in front of the telly.

If life as joyful gift is at the heart of the Kingdom that Jesus proclaims then it is not surprising that meals — open to all comers — were the scandalous enactment of it, and one particular meal was made by him the focus of all that he was, and remains the focus of those who seek to live his way since. To that we shall come in a moment.

Prayer

From the meal to prayer. If the shared meal with all comers was the most vivid and offensive embodiment of the Kingdom, then prayer was its life blood. At the heart of the message of the Kingdom was the experience of life as pure grace and gift, moment by moment, a sense of being utterly treasured and cherished without effort or achievement or success releasing in the individual the capacity to treasure and cherish others. In any community that clings to this, there comes into being a benign circle of affirmation liberating both a sense of celebration and joyfulness, and paradoxically allowing the dark and damaged parts of peoples lives to come to the surface to receive acceptance. It is a strange truth in the mysterious chemistry of spirituality, that men and women can only reveal their pain and weep over their sins and the damage they have received and meted out to others, in conditions of the most total acceptance. The judgement of God, which is always the most painful healing, is released in the human soul when the love of God is most immediate and present. It is this truth that renders the Church's postures of moral judgement on the sins of others, so extraordinarily barren and unproductive, for they never reach the heart.

But how can such experiences be sustained? A sense of life and one another and the world and all creatures and all existence as gift is not an uncommon religious experience. It is a rare and damaged person who has not — perhaps just fleetingly — broken out of the narrow confines of the all-consuming self to experience, perhaps through nature, or through the devotion of a friend, a glimpse of the goodness and the *givenness* of all things. These moments of natural wonder and thanksgiving are profoundly healing when they come unbidden and they ought not to be despised by those who regard themselves as professionally religious. However, can such insights be sustained or do they become simply ice cream in the sun, soon to melt and disappear under the fierce rays of our competitive grasping earn-life-for-yourself culture where we are set one against the other in the struggle for survival? In this kind of climate it is very hard for grace to survive.

The experience of life as God's good gift to be received, savoured and shared can only be sustained as we stretch beyond the natural but fleeting experiences of thankfulness to the one who is the Giver, the one whom Jesus daringly called *'Abba'*. Daring because it was intimate, personal, immediate and brought God right into the centre of the human heart. *Abba* more than anything else denotes the intimate aliveness of God to Jesus. He of course was born into, nurtured, lived and taught in a highly charged religious culture. God and the things of God dominated every tiny aspect of life. In our haemorrhaged secular world it is perhaps less easy to see prayer as central and sustaining for every moment of life, and may require a persistent doggedness and a kind of nakedness of faith to go on naming the Name even if it is only in the depths of our own heart. For the man Jesus the experience of relatedness to *Abba* was foundational, the source and inspiration of every moment he lived, every word he spoke, every thing he did and the root of his sense of life as good and given. Each moment was rooted in *Abba* — dear Father. And the Father who cherishes Jesus is not simply his father but 'our Father', the Father of all who cherishes and treasures and gives life to all, all things and all creatures, and says that at the root of all things there is goodness.

They asked for help in praying. And the prayer he taught them perhaps takes us nearer to the Kingdom than anything else. When you pray, he said, say:

'Father, may your name be held holy.' The source of all life as gift and grace is God as Father, who though intimately alive to us as *Abba*, is yet also infinitely other — holy. To hold the name holy is not only to find a source and refer-

ence point infinitely beyond, but also to revere and honour and respect all life itself as his gift.

'*Your Kingdom come.*' The second petition of the prayer is as we should expect from Jesus, a prayer for the Kingdom — that the Reign of God the Father of all may break through the bruised and defended consciousness of men and women ensnared in our own endless systems of self-justification, our guilt, our failure, our mutual hostility and violence. The Kingdom prayed for is God's and is itself a gift now 'at hand', coming into the world and radically reversing all worldly values and systems.

'*Give us each day our daily bread.*' The first word of the third petition places us in total dependence on the Giver. May we know and experience consciously each day life as dependency and gift through the receiving of bread the staff of life. And the gift and the bread is just for today — each day for that day as it was in the desert — curing us of the mistrust, the worm of anxiety that hoards and wonders and fears, and robs both ourselves and others of life as joyful gift, as we systematically (i.e. through systems) steal from others what does not belong to us.

Only when we have acknowledged the Giver, longed for the Kingdom and received the gift is it necessary to turn to ourselves. We are following Luke's simpler and earlier version: '*Forgive us our sins for we ourselves forgive each one who is in debt to us.*' Gradually it becomes apparent to the believer who has begun to know and live life as gift and gratefulness how constant and total is the alienation and the distortion of the self which has tried to live independently of the Giver in pursuit of self-justification and self-gratification at every turn. A kind of shame is born — we have trampled on others personally, collectively, internationally. So there is evoked repentance, *metanoia* — a struggle to make a total about-turn, a reversal and turning back to the Giver — 'Lord have mercy'. In the light of forgiveness received, we are not just willing but able — released — to offer it abundantly to others as it has been offered to us.

And so to the inevitable future of this life of the Kingdom. *'And do not put us to the test'.* The final phrase of the prayer simply acknowledges the logic of life in the Kingdom lived faithfully: it will lead to the most profound offense. Testing and trial must come. We do not wish it. We love life, this good gift. May the trial be put off, postponed, somehow if possible avoided, for Father, this life is so good.

This kind of praying is a far cry from what goes on in many services or prayer meetings where we think we are heard 'for our much speaking'. The dominant note is one of resting — longing, waiting, receiving — in John's word 'abiding'. A new kind of conviction is born — life is gift felt at the depth of ourselves. The business of prayer is to sustain this against all around in a culture which shrieks the opposite.

Miracle

In Jesus's programme of announcing the Kingdom, parable was the evocative tool jerking the listener awake so that they may see; the meal was its lived embodiment; prayer was the sustaining power; miracle was the sign of its arrival in a material world. Something at least needs to be said of miracle if only because miracles occur again and again in the New Testament and they are part of any search for the Kingdom as it was in Jesus. However, Christian history has been so bedevilled by the wrong understanding of miracle using them as 'proof' of the divinity of Jesus that it is almost impossible to see straight.

The first thing that needs to be remembered is that this is the world of the New Testament. Their understanding was simple: on the one hand there is the power of evil, the power of Satan to destroy, disfigure, maim, make leprous and blind. On the other hand there is the power of God to heal, to forgive, to raise up, to bring life. They knew nothing of our 'scientific' world view, where the material world is governed by 'laws of nature' which 'miracles' break. 'As for whether natural laws are being broken or respected, nobody has a thought about that, neither Jesus nor his auditors, participating in the event by approving or disapproving of it. The miraculous element that finds expression in Jesus is not a point for his opponents or for his supporters; but what does count is the ultimate interpretation of what both parties alike experience.'[14] Following from this it is quite clear from the earliest strata of tradition, that Jesus clearly did do some healing acts. However it is equally clear that in the course of time, among the highly-charged Galilean community, his powers as exorcist and healer became exaggerated, and in the early Church, miracle stories developed from the perspective of faith in Jesus as God's Messiah and particularly God's eschatological prophet. This is not the place to go into the question of the historical content of the miracle story tradition in the Gospels. Nor is it the most important question about the miracle tradition. Instead of getting hung up on the question: did the miracles happen literally as described in the Gospels? we need to use them as picture stories — allowing the imagination to penetrate them until they reveal our own life situations. A favourite of mine is the cure of the paralytic in Mark chapter two. This is how Mark describes it:

> When he returned to Capernaum some time later, word went round that he was back; and so many people collected that there was no room left, even in front of the door. He was preaching the word to them when some people came bringing him a paralytic carried by four men, but as the crowd made it impossible to get the man to him, they stripped the roof over the place where Jesus was; and when they had made an opening, they lowered the stretcher on which the paralytic lay. Seeing their faith, Jesus said to the paralytic 'My child, your sins are forgiven.' Now some scribes were sitting there, and they thought to themselves, 'How can this man talk like that? He is blaspheming. Who can forgive sins but God?' Jesus, inwardly aware that this was what they were thinking, said to them, 'Why do you have these thoughts in your hearts? Which of these is easier: to say to the paralytic, "Your sins are forgiven" or to say, "Get up,

pick up your stretcher and walk"? But to prove to you that the Son of Man has authority on earth to forgive sins,' — he said to the paralytic — 'I order you: get up, pick up your stretcher, and go off home.' And the man got up picked up his stretcher at once and walked out in front of everyone, so that they were all astounded and praised God saying, 'We have never seen anything like this' (Mark 2:1–12).

Let's allow our imagination to enter into this familiar story. For years we may suppose this 'paralytic' had lain, crippled and bent at some street corner begging for alms. A victim of God's punishment, condemned, sneered at and abandoned — regarded by all as a worthless thing. His body was crippled and paralysed, but God knows what kind of damage he had sustained inside in terms of low self-esteem and inner self-contempt. The Gospel describes him simply as a 'paralytic'. No name, no movement, no person. The extent of the inner hurt make his physical disability almost insignificant. He cannot believe. Life has no prospect of change. He is damned into hopelessness for ever. But he is brought by men who do believe. The small flat-roofed Palestinian house is tight-packed, bulging at the door. No room at this inn. It is a moment for rapid, even aggressive decision. With determined movement this bent dead thing is hauled up the stairs, across the roof, and lies immobile while faith in the Kingdom drives them to wrench open the gaping hole. Inside all eyes look up. Slowly the man is lowered, lovingly, down. The people make space shuffling back against one another until the stretcher reaches the dusty floor. This bent twisted 'paralytic' lies at the feet of Jesus. Every cranny of darkness within exposed to the light above. Agony. Unbearable attention. Trapped. Waves of shame and hurt. And then the words: 'My child —- *my child* — your sins are forgiven!' The effect is extraordinary. The darkness accepted and washed away. Forgiven! Forgiven. The word somehow believed, and said and sung and said a million times again afterwards in the new moving life. 'My child — forgiven.' Flowing from this is the healing.

A command to move: 'Get up, pick up your stretcher and walk.' The one flows from the other. Forgiveness releases the movement.

Mark may have had a particular theological purpose in placing this story so early in his Gospel. The power of Jesus as the Christ confronting evil, and the underlining of Jesus as the Son of God who can forgive sins. But for us, while learning these theological lessons, the benefit may be in the imaginative detail. As we enter imaginatively into the story, and what a good story it is, it is not difficult for us to see ourselves and others in this 'paralytic'; to recognise our moments of frozen immobility; to see there our sense of low self-esteem; to imagine in him our hatred and envy of others who change, move, shine, adapt and progress. Perhaps we know too the agony of being exposed to the truth of what's going on in us, and recognise in the four friends our real friends who are determined that we face up to ourselves. And can we hear the words of Jesus Christ? 'My child your sins are forgiven.' For most of us it takes a lifetime to receive these words in the depths of ourselves, and believe them so deeply that we too can pick up our stretchers, our props and crutches and the pathetic cushioning bric-a-brac that we surround ourselves with, and walk forward into a life that is totally new discarding the stretcher in the nearest bin.

The miracle speaks of our lives now, cramped and frozen, and conveys the possibilities of faith in the Kingdom. When men and women in communities grasp hold of life as God's precious gift and rest in that, remarkable things do happen. People get back in touch with their life, their bodies, the earth, their neighbour, and begin to see it all — all as a gift. Healing then happens. This may include things apparently quite 'miraculous'. Above all the miracles of Jesus are signs that the Kingdom is about the *material* world underlining the unity of the material and spiritual — a fundamental Jewish insight.

Where has the search led us? In the teaching of Jesus, against the background of factional division, we have seen the Kingdom evoked and made potentially present to all through the story, the meal, the practice of prayer, and the power of healing. It is his lived conviction of life as gift and treasure coming constantly from the hands of the Father who treasures and cherishes all irrespective of any human consideration. The only condition to enter this arena of grace is the willingness to receive it — pure gift. Attempts to make your own life worthy or to secure your life as possession, indeed to grasp at anything as possession rather than gift is what will undo you, blocking you off from the life of the Kingdom, creating barriers of suspicion and envy at what others have got and therefore sowing division. For Jesus, to regard life as a personal possession secured by effort is the very root of sin. It denies the gift and it denies the Giver and at the end of the day it is futile. By this approach we will make ourselves incurably anxious, for death lurks constantly, threatening inevitably to rob us and tear from our grasp everything we have so painstakingly built up.

Crisis

Such a lived conviction was inevitably sharply divisive and took him to the final moment of trial, which his prayer had anticipated. As his mother had foretold, he had raised up the poor who had nothing to offer but their need, the poor who had hung on his stories, been healed through his forgiveness, had shared in his meals and stumblingly learnt to join in his prayer. They received the gift. And the message of the Kingdom had sent the rich and powerful empty away gnashing their teeth, tearing their robes, bent on destroying him. Their position and authority, protected by an ornate religious system of approval and condemnation which governed every tiny detail of personal and public life, was being put at risk and undermined. To them nothing less than the Jewish religion as they understood and interpreted it, was at stake. Jesus had to die in order to preserve the nation.

So the crisis came. If the Kingdom is life as gift received moment by moment, daily bread, from the Giver, then that conviction must mean a readiness open handed in trusting faith when the moment comes to return life — back to the One who gives all. Jesus was ready when the moment came to return this gift to the Father. The New Testament is quite explicit here: it does not speak of Jesus having his life torn from him, body kicking and screaming or limp in sullen protest. It speaks of The Man who knew the hour had come, who prayed in the darkness of the garden 'Your will be done', and who at the end yielded up his life. In death Jesus became the Kingdom. In death he lived out, exemplified, showed to the uttermost his conviction that life was gift to be received from the Giver or taken away by the Giver, and life could only be found in trusting that Giver. It was in his death that Jesus became the Kingdom. The victim triumphed. Death was robbed of its power. This man put his faith not in his own will to life, or power of survival, but in the life-Giver, even as life ebbed away. Not knowing of the future, but trusting in that life-Giver he gave back life to the One from whom it had come. Some of the ancient paintings of the crucifixion portray Jesus' head resting on the cross beam. It is appropriate. In death as it had been moment by moment in life, and transcending his death and his life was this resting trust in the life-Giver. And Christian faith mysteriously and stubbornly asserts that life *was* given back beyond death, in the glory of the resurrection.

This may all sound rather beyond us — and of course quite literally, it is. In the crucifixion we see the monumental and triumphant struggle of faith in the Kingdom. Jesus of Nazareth, now the Christ, has pioneered the route of faith right through the barrier that had seemed to negate all faith. And the Church's stubborn and joyful conviction of his resurrection vindicates this faith and provides the courage to follow the same way.

Eucharist

It may indeed all seem rather beyond us. And yet there is a place where we are invited repeatedly, day after day, week after week, to enter into the way of the Kingdom life until it shapes and moulds our whole mental and spiritual orientation, percolating deeper and deeper into our consciousness. It is a most familiar down-to-earth place. Where else but the meal? And one particular meal that Jesus invested on the last night of his life with new meaning.

The Last Supper, or Eucharist, or Mass, is always a kind of holy theatre — a re-enactment and re-staging once again of that last special meal. On that occasion it was the Passover meal that he celebrated, the meal which gathers up and focuses the essence of the Jewish story, his own inherited story. On that particular Passover night, the night he was betrayed, Jesus enacts a new Passover, a release from the doomed and anxious finality of self-justification into the eternal promise of life as given. He takes the bread and pours out wine, his life, his body and blood, and gives it back to the Father. He offers a new way of life for the world: this is my body given, this is my blood shed — do this in remembrance of me. Before them and with those bewildered poor and us bewildered poor too, he lives out to the end his faith in the Kingdom.

Of course it was bloody agony. By theology or time or art we cannot soften or sentimentalise what the Gospel writers show was a hellish struggle. To surrender this precious gift is no easy thing. It means sweat and tears. Jesus above all has revelled and rejoiced in it, felt the power of it — lived it. Nevertheless in Gethsemane come the words 'not my will but thine be done'. Jesus surrenders his life not knowing any more than any person can know of the future in the face of death — but *believing*. And so he becomes the very life of the Kingdom and in Paul's words 'a life-giving spirit' (1 Cor 15:45).

The Eucharist then becomes the place where his life becomes present to us again and again and again. By eating and drinking his body and blood we enter into the way of the Kingdom: poor and empty ourselves we struggle to receive the gift, give to others, and prepare to give back our life to the One from whom it comes at that moment when we too shall die. So death is robbed of its sting, its final power to destroy. Life is ultimately not our own, it belongs to Another who dwells in us. In and around and through this whole experience of Eucharist there comes present to us this Other — the life-giving spirit of Jesus alive to us once again as we break the bread. The Eucharist becomes then the place of resurrection. In the house at Emmaus, he was known to them in 'the breaking of the bread' (Luke 24:35). The Eucharist takes us to the heart of the message of the Kingdom of God. He *is* known to us too, in the breaking of the bread.

The Search Ended — and Begun . . .

From this summary of some key features of Jesus's preaching and living of the Kingdom, there arises the question from the previous chapter: In what sense can we claim that this Jesus has fulfilled the Jewish hope sketched out there? Clearly expectations were disappointed. On the Emmaus road they said, 'Our own hope had been that he would be the one to set Israel free' (Luke 24:21). Judaism asks how can the Kingdom have come and the world be so manifestly unredeemed? Christians have always insisted on the paradoxical nature of the Kingdom: yes it has come, and at the same time, not yet in its fullness. Through this man the open secret of the Kingdom has been revealed and laid bare, through his life, and particularly through his death — and his resurrection. God has raised him up, the first of the new age. To use John's language, light has shone in our darkness 'and the darkness has not overcome it'.

But the darkness remains — sometimes total blackness. The Christian hope is that the ancient hope of Israel for a Kingdom coming in history, of justice and material blessedness, is potentially fulfilled in and through this Jesus. The way through has been blazed by one man with the invitation to all men and women to follow behind.

Quite explicitly, in the teaching of Jesus the social morality at the heart of the Jewish law potentially came to fruition in history. The poor are raised up. In his message and action all men and women were equally graced and treasured by God and by implication therefore the right of the rich to possess and appropriate life and land and power and wealth for themselves as possession was fundamentally challenged and ultimately proclaimed blasphemy and idolatry. The seeds of the courage of later Christians, particularly in our own century and time, to insist on the earth and land as shared gift were sown. The promise in the beatitudes is that the poor of the Kingdom 'shall inherit *the earth*' (Matt 5:4).

Secondly, the ancient universal hope of Israel given to Abraham at the beginning of the Old Testament and expressed through Isaiah, the 'originator of a theology of world history', at the end of the Old Testament period, was born into reality. The hope of the whole earth was incarnated in this man. We see Jesus constantly extending the promises of God beyond the borders of Judaism to include in, the Samaritan, the Centurion, the Canaanite woman, the thief, the brigand, the tax collector, the harlot. Again and again in the Gospels the barriers of exclusive claims to relationship with God are trampled down. At the feast of the Kingdom of God they will come from *every* race and tribe and people and nation and class and colour — and this hope was made flesh in Jesus. Paul — the apostle to the Gentiles — faithful to this life-giving spirit of Jesus breaks through the barriers of Judaism to the whole inhabited earth. That is why his rather strange writings about no longer needing circumcision (the mark of the Jew) for life in God's Kingdom is so fundamental. The promises of God are for *all*. The universal hope of the prophets has arrived: a new world of one God and Father of all his cherished children and treasured earth has dawned.

So a new history is begun. A new dynamic is released called the spirit of Jesus known centrally in the Eucharist. Jesus has brought to an end the era of the long search and ushered in a new world of lived gratitude. The ancient hope of the Jews is fulfilled and yet the whole creation also waits in longing. The New Testament insists that we are saved in hope, and are called ourselves to search hard for this Kingdom. It is this search in our own lives and our own history that will be the focus in the second and third parts.

PART TWO

IN SEARCH OF OUR SELVES

The longest journey is always the inward one. The journey home to find oneself takes a whole lifetime; and perhaps more.
Jürgen Moltmann

Chapter 3: The Personal Search

In Part One we have been laying foundations, exploring definitions. We have seen that faith is a search for the promised future; that in and through the Hebrew story, a vision of the Reign of God is revealed; that through Jesus, life is offered as gift and grace for all. The search is ended. The Kingdom of God, claims the New Testament, has dawned in and through this man. The first letter of John tries to express this extraordinary truth:

> Something which has existed since the beginning,
> that we have heard,
> and we have seen with our own eyes;
> that we have watched
> and touched with our hands:
> the Word, who is life —
> this is our subject.
> That life was made visible:
> we saw it and we are giving our testimony,
> telling you of the eternal life
> which was with the Father and has been made visible
> to us (1 John 1:1–2).

Thus they whispered it in the synagogues and shouted it from the house tops! The day had dawned. We heard it, saw it, touched it, felt it! The language of the New Testament tries to convey that something had arrived that blew their world apart. God himself had met them.

What of us and our world? So much of this biblical material has been tamed and absorbed over the centuries into our history, and become familiar and comfortable by time and repetition, taking its place as part of the cultural wallpaper although now badly torn and shredded. However, though we express it differently, we are as restless for this Kingdom as any synagogue of Jews praying the Kaddish prayer. The sharp question is: how do these remote stories and the Church which tries to hold and live them, engage with our personal and social lives *now*. Put personally, is there a way whereby I too can enter into the search and discover the Kingdom?

Jesus may be the end of the long search, but he is also the beginning of the search for every believer and for every society. Paradoxically the search is both ended and yet ever beginning again, for there is no short cut, no instant access to the life of the Kingdom. Like Abraham each has to set out 'not knowing where we are going', though because of the Hebrew story, and because of what Jesus revealed, Christians hold that the trail right through to the heart of God is opened up by him whom we see as 'the pioneer and perfector of faith' (Heb 12:12). Others — the communion of saints — have followed, widening the path, clearing the route. And yet, however much the trail has been marked out with signposts erected, and One of us has blazed it, nevertheless each must personally make his or her own individual journey. Each of us must write our own version of the good news. The Gospel according to Sarah, Peter, Frank, David, Lorna, Mary, Bill, Kate . . . has to be discovered, for each of us is different, shaped and formed and moulded by the particular circumstances and situations into which we were born and in which we grew up. Each has our own very particular story to tell, and no one can tell it for us. It is out of the raw material of that story, those hopes and fears and longings and regrets and triumphs that God, slowly and painstakingly, builds the life of his Kingdom.

In this second part, our concern is the *personal* search for the Kingdom. The Kingdom, as we shall see in the third part is much more than individual experience, it is essentially corporate, involving politics as much as prayer. Nevertheless, the way into the life of the Kingdom in our particular culture with its emphasis upon the individual, usually, though not always, begins in the arena of personal experience. And it is clear that I can give little that is constructive either to my neighbour or my community until I have begun to face the riddle of my own life. Those who rush headlong into social activism, perhaps as a way — unconsciously — of avoiding personal questions can simply end up unwittingly inflicting their unresolved needs and tensions on to others. This is not to say that Christians as they grapple with questions of faith, should retreat from society into a kind of isolated inner world of private exploration. Social engagement and personal quest go hand in hand and each contributes to the other. But it is clear that in the lives of the saints, there is often an initial period of painful searching before the new self 'created in Christ Jesus' (Eph 2:10) is sufficiently formed to engage with the questions of God's Kingdom in the world.

The Bible itself indicates this kind of pattern of personal quest and trial before the Kingdom is announced. After his baptism in the Jordan, Jesus is driven into the wilderness to face the wild beasts, symbolic of the inner struggle and question of his own identity. Paul Tillich writes: 'He is alone, facing the whole earth and sky, the wild beasts around him and within him, he himself the battlefield for divine and demonic forces . . . this is what happens in our solitude, we meet ourselves not as ourselves but as the battlefield for creation and destruction, for God and the demons.'[1]

Paul of Tarsus seems to have undergone a similar wilderness testing. In his letter to the Galatians he writes (Gal 1:17) of going immediately after his dramatic conversion not to Jerusalem to meet the other apostles and find reconciliation, but to Arabia. And what is Arabia but the desert?

A Threefold Exodus Pattern

The pattern that provides the framework for understanding Jesus's wilderness experience, is the Exodus event itself. The original Israel of God fled from the oppression of Egypt through the waters, into the emptiness of the desert, with the promise of the land held out ahead of them. There they became a people, forged into an instrument for God's purpose of salvation for all. The desert was his crucible, his place of creation, where Israel is built into a people strong enough to enter the land and to confront the gods of the nations. But it was not just a framework for interpreting Jesus' wilderness experience. This Exodus event offers a fundamental pattern and shape for all searching for the Kingdom. It has a threefold structure. (1). There is a promise of a new ideal world where God will transform everything and this motivates the flight from evil and oppression. (2). But in between the promised future and the oppressive past is a desert, an empty wild place which somehow has to be travelled through. Extraordinarily, this desert far from being a place of death, is where, against all expectation, life is given. (3). From it, the traveller emerges ready and able to face destructive powers. This pattern is archetypal for the personal journey and this gives the Exodus story its peculiar importance. They led the way that needs to be followed in the most intimate and personal terms.

In this Exodus pattern, what we are talking about is conversion. In his book on the personal quest, *Soul Making, The Desert Way of Spirituality*, Alan Jones reminds us that conversion is not a once for all event 'but a way of psychological and spiritual formation that takes a lifetime'.[2] And he reflects that the mystics often thought in terms of a threefold pattern of conversion. The first conversion is to joy, hope and a new beginning. The second stage is an experience of hope betrayed when everything seems to fall apart, and yet through it there is given a new energy and power. The third stage is a deepening of contemplation leading to action and service in the world.

Each of these three stages are key moments in the Gospel story. First, the disciples respond to the call of Jesus leaving everything to follow him into a new life. But then, at the cross, hope is betrayed — 'Our own hope had been that he would be the one to set Israel free' — though through the resurrection they are given power to live from a new source. Pentecost and the gift of the Spirit is the third stage, involving a deeper experience of the life of God leading to mission, the engaging with the powers of the world.

This threefold Exodus, Gospel pattern, offers a framework for understanding our own discipleship and search for the Kingdom. Of course we come to faith in very diverse ways. These three stages of conversion should not be understood rigidly nor do they always follow chronologically. Jones encourages us to think of them in 'spiral'[3] rather than linear terms, the three stages repeating themselves again and again. There are times of epiphany, when we sense we are met and called forward and the world is lit up with new possibility. There are times of betrayal and darkness through which faith paradoxically can be deepened. And there are times of a more consistent resting in God when we can turn away from self-concern to engage openly and honestly with others.

Sometimes one stage predominates and people get stuck distorting and making lopsided the life of discipleship. For some, almost the only experience they know is the second stage, a wrestling with unasked for fear and doubt: the only symbol that speaks is the Cross, there is darkness over the whole land constantly with scarcely a glimmer of resurrection. Others cling to the first stage, fearing to look deeper, and working hard to be joyful. Others are dismissive of any time spent on issues of personal faith, the only thing that matters is social action. Jones makes a plea for all three, particularly the second, to be part of our understanding of evangelism. Experience varies but in our personal quests for the life of the Kingdom this ancient threefold pattern offers a framework for self-understanding and points to a fullness of experience. In this second part we shall make it the basis of our exploration.

Thomas Merton: a Paradigm

In such discussion it is easy to get swamped in vague generalities or sentimental abstractions. We need a sharp focus. The experience of conversion can only be understood through the individual stories of specific people. To provide that sharp focus I have chosen to reflect on the very particular story of one man, the American Trappist monk, Thomas Merton, and to use his life as a kind of model or paradigm of the personal search, the way of the threefold conversion. To those who have never heard of him it will become clear in the next chapter who Merton was, and I hope something of his extraordinary significance for twentieth-century Christianity will become apparent. I have chosen to look at his experience as we have it from his writings and journals not because he is one of the most influential religious figures in our age, nor because of the simple power of his writing, but because Merton's story in all its vividness follows, as he recognised himself, the threefold pattern of the Jewish Exodus/Christian Gospel motif. There was a flight from 'the world' to the promise of something radically new. Then a long period of painful re-creation in the desert of the spirit. Thirdly, in the sixties, a deeper living of the contemplative life and a turning again to 'the world'. As we reflect on his experience, we see a man being refashioned in the midst of our contemporary society. With rare depth he struggled with the question of what it means to believe and be a human being in our particular age, and he emerged victorious with truth to tell. Merton was a pioneer, his story offers us profound understanding of the search for the Kingdom in the twentieth century.

Following the threefold pattern I have divided his story into three sections. First, his life and flight from the world into the monastery which he entered in 1941. Second his life and writings in the crisis 'desert' period of the early 1950s. Thirdly, his deepening contemplation and turning to the life of the 'world' in the later 1950s and 60s. In between each there is a reflection on the pattern of experience that he recounts.

Thomas Merton died on 10 December 1968. When his early autobiography was published in 1947 not long after he had entered the monastery of Our Lady of Gethsemani, Kentucky, the novelist Graham Greene wrote: 'It is a rare pleasure to read an autobiography with a pattern and a meaning valid for all of us.'[4] It is that pattern and meaning, extending beyond the early years into the 1950s and 60s, that provides the focus for this search. Finally, it may seem strange to choose as an exemplar of the personal search an American Catholic monk. Very few are called to that kind of life, so how can his life speak to ours? However, if at first his story seems remote and distant or even forbidding, then persevere. The outer details of his life are of course important, they are his particular frame and context and we must understand them as fully as possible. But it is the *inner* struggle and growth that matters, and that we share in common. What we see in Merton with rare depth and clarity is one man's struggle as he put it himself to save 'my sinful soul'[5] in the midst of the conditions of the twentieth-century world, and to share that struggle with others. Despite the outward and obvious differences, what we can see through him and his story, is ourselves and our world writ large, in all our lostness and potential glory. And through his story we are offered new depths of understanding of the Gospel of Jesus Christ.

So to this story, and reflection on it, we turn. In order to grasp something of the depth of his later struggle of faith particularly in the desert period of the early 1950s, it is important to immerse ourselves in the detail of his early life leading up to his entry into Gethsemani in 1941.

Chapter 4: The Road to Eden

Thomas Merton was born in France on 31st January 1915, the son of Ruth and Owen Merton. His parents were both artists, and had met in Paris as students. Ruth was an American from Long Island in New York state, and Owen a New Zealander, though he had left New Zealand at the age of seventeen to finish his education in England at the Canterbury School of Art.

Ideals of Perfection

Not long before Tom was born the Mertons had taken a small house in southern France — in the Eastern Pyrenees — in the little town of Prades, in order to paint and live a simple idealistic life:

> 'Father wanted to get some place where he could settle in France, and raise a family, and paint, and live on practically nothing, because we had practically nothing to live on.'[1]

Soon though, the dream was to be interrupted by the growing menace of war and the family crossed the Atlantic to Long Island to Ruth's family home, and set up their own home at Flushing. There little Tom grew up, and at the age of three his brother John Paul — 'a child with a much serener nature than mine'[2] — was born. The picture Merton paints of his mother in his autobiography is significant: she was a woman with high ideals and demanding expectations of her little son. She sent off for a progressive method of education and proceeded to teach the child herself. Tom remembers being sent to bed at the age of five for spelling 'which' without the first 'h'.

I remember brooding about this as an injustice. 'What do they think I am anyway? After all, I was still only five years old.'[3]

Later he writes:

Mother wanted me to be an independent, and not to run with the herd. I was to be original, individual, I was to have a definite character and ideals of my own. I was not to be an article thrown together, on the common bourgeois pattern, on everybody else's assembly line.[4]

It is clear that this fastidious intellectual and rather severe mother, with her 'numerous and haunting ideals of perfection'[5] bred in the little boy a deep sense of himself as unsatisfactory and even unworthy. There is something lonely and bleak about the child aged five surrounded by the desk and blackboard at home, and faced with the demanding parent. Merton remembers he invented a friend — Jack, with a dog called Doolittle. Nevertheless it was not an unhappy period, and he was able to enjoy for a short time the companionship of his little, more serene, brother John Paul, before tragically the family was broken up.

A Weight of Sadness

While Tom was still small his mother was taken to hospital with cancer of the stomach, never to see her children again. Tom was never taken to the hospital as she feared it might make him 'morbid'. And then one day, at the tender age of six, he received from her a letter — the only letter he ever received from her — written in 'confusing' language, informing him that she was going to die:

I took the note out under the maple tree in the back yard, and worked over it, until I had made it all out, and had gathered what it really meant. And a tremendous weight of sadness and depression settled on me. It was not the grief of a child, with pangs of sorrow and many tears. It had something of the heavy perplexity and gloom of adult grief, and was therefore all the more of a burden . . . [6]

Later Merton wrote of being taken to the hospital on the actual day of her death. He was not allowed to enter the building, but waited for a long time outside listening to the drops of rain falling on the roof of the car:

The sky was heavy with mist and smoke, and the sweet sick smell of hospital and gas-house mingled with the stuffy smell of the automobile.[7]

The death of his mother began Merton's wanderings, and however 'severe' she may have been, the loss of her at so early an age ensured that the foundations of his life were scarred by a deep wound, that was soon to be repeated.

Within a month the family split up with Tom, who was old enough to go, and his father setting off in search of somewhere to settle where he could paint, leaving John Paul behind in Long Island with Ruth's parents. First father and son went to Cape Cod, then back to Long Island, then to Bermuda, then back to Long Island again. There Tom was temporarily left while Owen went to France, soon to return to take young nine-year-old Tom with him.

On being told they were going to France, Tom was against it, fiercely resisting the idea of being uprooted from his friends and familiar surroundings to accompany his father to the strange land of his birth, so different from the brash America of the 1920s. But after the crossing of the Loire as they travelled south, he had the strange sense that he was 'home', and he immediately fell in love with this land so saturated with the rich culture of Catholic medi-aeval Europe. 'I was to live and drink from the fountains of the Middle Ages.'[8] Eventually they reached the town of their destination, St Antonin in southern France, an almost perfectly preserved mediaeval town at the centre of which was the church, the church which as he later wrote gave meaning to the whole, and forced you 'in spite of yourself, to be at least a virtual contemplative!'[9]

The landscape, architecture and history of Catholic France made a profound and lasting impression on him, he sensed intuitively the wholeness under God of mediaeval culture. Personally, though, France was to be a place where his loneliness was deepened. His first school was the elementary at St Antonin where he sat with children of 'workmen and peasants'[10] and was happy. Soon however he was sent off as a boarder to the Lycee in a nearby town and there, due to the strangeness and the crude boyish bullying of the first few days he knew consciously for the first time: 'the pangs of desolation and emptiness and abandonment.'[11] Although he endured it well enough Merton hated the Protestant Lycee which seemed to him so far from the spirit of his idealised Catholic France.

Soon though, in 1928, he was free. His father returned from England to announce they were leaving France for good and moving to London — to Ealing, to live with his father's sister, the very English Aunt Maud. In no time Merton was kitted out and packed off to a traditional English preparatory school, Ripley Court, in Surrey. From there he progressed to Oakham, a minor public school in the East Midlands where he excelled at Rugby, edited the school magazine, and learnt from the Anglican chaplain 'Buggy' Jerwood that charity in St Paul's letter to the Corinthians meant being a decent English gentleman.

It was while at Oakham, that once again Merton had to go through the pain of bereavement. While on holiday in Scotland, he received a telegram through a phone call which indicated that his father whom he adored was dying of a brain tumour in London. Merton recalls receiving the news:

I hung up the receiver and the bottom dropped out of my stomach. I walked up and down in the silent and empty house. I sat down in one of the big leather chairs in the smoking room. There was nobody there. There

> was nobody in the whole huge house. I sat there in the
> dark unhappy room, unable to think, unable to move,
> with all the innumerable elements of my isolation crowd-
> ing upon me from every side: without a home, without
> a family, without a country, without a father, apparently
> without any friends, without any interior peace or confi-
> dence or light or understanding of my own . . . [12]

In fact it was a year before Owen died. From the first page
of the autobiography it is clear that Merton was devoted
to his footloose artistic father, a deep bond had developed
between them, and when death came, the wound of grief
was raw and very deep.

Merton was now an orphan. However, his natural
vitality, together with his popularity ensured that he over-
came the immediate depression, and the gaping hole of
loneliness and emptiness within was buried.

His godfather, Tom Bennett, an old friend of his father
was made his guardian. Tom and his french wife Iris lived
a sophisticated life in London's Harley Street, and here
Merton spent his holidays. Frequently they travelled to
France and visited art galleries, exhibitions, and something
that was later to become a passion of Merton's — the
movies. Through the Bennetts, Merton was introduced into
a wider world than the rather cramped and restrained way
of life of Aunt Maud, Ripley Court and Oakham. He read
widely (Lawrence, Joyce, Hemingway) and developed a
cynical and critical detachment from the complacent smug-
ness of English middle-class life. He felt too that the death
of his father had removed both a profound security and
an important sense of restraint in his rapidly maturing
adolescent life. The world was now his . . . 'and with my
intelligence and five sharp senses I would rob all its treasures and rifle its coffers and empty them all.'[13]

From Oakham, he won an exhibition to Clare College
Cambridge. In the nine-month gap between school and
university, he visited Italy. It was in Rome, fascinated by
the Byzantine mosaics, that this cultured, well-read, sen-
sual young man 'began to find out something of Who this

person is that men call Christ'.[14] Again, as at St Antonin, it was the architecture of the place that was the mediator of the sense of God. Merton felt drawn to the churches of Rome, 'and thus without knowing anything about it I became a pilgrim'.[15] And then one night in his hotel room, the first profound religious experience of his life occurred:

> I was in my room. It was night. The light was on. Suddenly it seemed to me that Father, who had now been dead more than a year was with me. The sense of his presence was as vivid and as real and as startling as if he had touched my arm or spoken to me . . . I was overwhelmed with a sudden and profound insight into the misery and corruption of my soul . . . and now I think for the first time in my whole life I really began to pray — praying not with my lips and with my intellect and my imagination, but praying out of the very roots of my life and of my being, and praying to the God I had never known, to reach down towards me out of his Darkness and to help me to get free of the thousand terrible things that held my will in their slavery.[16]

Clearly in this experience, some of the buried grief about his father surfaced, and with it an overwhelming sense of his own loneliness and emptiness. Here Merton writes of the vivid contrast that is the clearest theme in the Seven Storey Mountain, and perhaps the secret of its extraordinary success: the contrast between the sickness and corruption and lostness of the contemporary world, with man enslaved in his own appetites within it, and the pure life of God reaching down 'out of his darkness to help me to get free . . .' It was this contrast, experienced ever more deeply as conflict in his soul that eventually drove him to the monastery to slam the door on the world, to be free as he thought, forever.

Cambridge

After a brief visit for a summer holiday in America, where he got himself a job for a few days as a barker on the front of a side-show at the World's Fair in Chicago, Merton went up to Cambridge in September 1933.

In the autobiography Merton writes bitterly of his wild unrestrained freshman's year:

> For me, with my blind appetites, it was impossible that I should not rush in and take a huge bite of this rotten fruit.[17]

Other than developing an acquaintance with the poetry of Dante through studying The Inferno he felt that 'all the rest was negative'.[18] Amidst his bitter account of the riotous life of late parties, and hangovers and womanising, two particular incidents stand out. One was 'a curt summons'[19] he received to come to London and see his guardian and explain his conduct. He writes that it was an extremely 'painful and distressing' occasion, and having been coldly asked to explain himself, he 'left me to writhe'.[20] The other involved the fate of a fellow undergraduate who was part of Merton's crowd. In the following year when Merton had left Cambridge, he heard that Mike had hanged himself from the pipes in the showers, and was found with 'his big hearty face black with the agony of strangulation.'[21]

There was a third incident not mentioned in the Seven Storey Mountain. In her biography Monica Furlong writes:

> One day Merton came to Andrew Winser and told him that he had 'got a girl into trouble'; he was deeply distressed by this. Later he was to mention this to friends at Columbia. The girl eventually bore his son, but both mother and son were killed, according to Ed Rice, during the London air raids.[22]

It is very difficult to know what effect this event had on Merton's life. In her Introduction, Furlong suggests that he 'suffered an excruciating sense of guilt and a conviction that a lifetime's expiation was demanded of him, and this certainly played an important part in taking him into the Trappists.'[23] It was, no doubt, the memory of this event, among others at Cambridge, that coloured his own account of his time there. He writes of a year of feverish energy and noise that masked despair — and moral corruption. But it was only to last a year. In the summer of 1934, while on holiday in America, Merton received a letter from his guardian, Tom Bennett, suggesting that he give up the idea of entering the Diplomatic Service, and that it would be useless to come back to Cambridge. Merton was not sorry to leave England. As the prospect of war cast its dark shadow over Europe — 'a sad and unquiet continent, full of forebodings'[24] — it was not difficult for him to project his own personal inner emptiness onto the society around him.

Columbia

From the start, Columbia University in New York where he enrolled the following year was different, and he felt at home. At Columbia he was to make friendships that lasted him the rest of his life, and profoundly influenced his direction. Columbia too was to be the place of a renewed search for a structure of meaning.

> The thing I always liked best about Columbia was the sense that the University was on the whole glad to turn me loose in its library, its classroom, and among its distinguished faculty . . . and I ended up being turned on like a pinball machine by Blake, Thomas Aquinas, Augustine, Eckhart, Coomaraswamy, Traherne, Hopkins, Maritain and the sacraments of the Catholic Church.[25]

And he became involved too with the National Students League (Communists) and demonstrations against war. Whilst this particular enthusiasm ebbed and flowed there was plenty of scope for the movies and jazz and late nights with his fraternity brothers in the 'noisy and expensive nightclubs'[26] in the cellars of 52nd Street.

In 1936 and 1937 his sense of being homeless in the world deepened when first his ebullient grandfather Pop died, and the following year Bonnemaman, Pop's wife. Once again death opened up old wounds and he found himself praying for Bonnemaman to live 'although I continued to think I believed in nothing'.[27] The deaths of these, his only grandparents whom he had loved and needed brought on a psychological crisis. He writes of a kind of nervous breakdown and an acute attack of vertigo in a high room in a New York hotel. He recovered but was afraid and chastened, and despite his friendships and success at Columbia more alone and hurt than he knew . . . 'beaten by this futile search for satisfaction'.[28]

There are many strands in Merton's turning from a life of vigorous and energetic and attractive self-indulgence, which masked though a profound loneliness which at times was near to despair, to eventually the life of a silent Trappist monk. And it was not sudden. One important strand was intellectual: through the writings of Etienne Gilson (*The Spirit of Mediaeval Philosophy*) he discovered a new concept of God — the power of 'Being itself'[29] — which moved him deeply and he found he had a profound desire 'to go to church'.[30] Aldous Huxley's work was important too, and through him he ransacked the University Library for books on Oriental Mysticism. The search focused on the writings of William Blake who was the subject of Merton's thesis. 'By the time the summer was over, I was to become conscious of the fact that the only way to live was to live in a world that was charged with the reality and presence of God.'[31]

A second strand was undoubtedly his friendships and the vigorous discussion they shared, discussion that often focused on the issue of becoming a Catholic.

A third strand was the influence of a small Indian Hindu monk, Dr Bramachari, who had come to America for the World Congress of Religions, and who paradoxically introduced him to the writings of St Augustine, and so opened his eyes to the depths of Catholic Spirituality.

Eventually the need to find a way of faith deeper than the dead rationalism of Protestantism, combined perhaps with echoes from his boyhood memories of Catholic culture in France drove him — for the first time — to Mass. On a bright Sunday morning, alone, he walked to the 'little brick Church of Corpus Christi',[32] and into 'a new world'.[33]

Thomas Merton was baptised on the 16th November 1938. After the Baptism, the Exorcism, the Signing of the Cross and the Salt of Wisdom on the tongue, he knelt in the confessional and 'one by one, that is species by species, as best I could, I tore out all those sins by their roots, like teeth'. The Service ended with Mass, and 'Christ was born in me — a new Bethlehem'.[34]

Merton never did anything by halves. The search for God must go to the limits. Before his baptism he had started to think of the priesthood, and even entering a monastery. But his new faith did nothing to dampen his extraordinary joie-de-vivre. As well as dates with girls, he was spending time writing and reading more than ever and friendships continued to blossom, particularly with one friend Bob Lax who suggested one day that Merton should want 'to become a saint'.[35]

The summer of 1939 was spent with Lax and others at a country cottage in the hills. All the time the menace of war was looming: it intensified his sense of the world as evil, and his own deep sense of guilt for his share in it:

> There was something else in my own mind — the recognition: 'I myself am responsible for this. My sins have done this. Hitler is not the only one who has started this war: I have my share in it too . . .'[36]

At times the guilt turns to contempt and self-disgust. It was at such a moment sitting on the floor of his flat in Perry St, New York, playing jazz records, eating breakfast and smoking cigarettes at one in the afternoon that quite suddenly the idea came to him: 'I am going to be a priest.'[37]

At both this point in his autobiography, and elsewhere Merton writes explicitly of his life in terms of a way into the new land, the promised land, out of Egypt — 'the land of human nature blinded and fettered by perversity and sin . . . '[38] where he 'persisted in living'.[39]

Even while he was involved in writing and getting reviews and articles published, and enjoying his talent for friendship, increasingly the search for a way of detaching himself from the world and finding some kind of deep peace and a home in God was engaging Merton's considerable spiritual energy. He actively considered which order he should join: the Jesuits, Franciscans, Dominicans, Benedictines? He had also heard from his friend Dan Walsh about the Cistercians of the Strict Observance (Trappists) but their austerity frightened and repelled him. Eventually it was arranged that he would join the Franciscans.

However the dream of religious bliss was soon to be shattered. As he prepared for the Franciscans, he was gripped by a sense that if he was to enter an Order he had to tell 'who I really was' and that meant again a full account of his past, and instinctively he knew that his dream of finding a home was finished. He recalls the train journey to the Franciscan seminary:

> It seemed a long, long journey as the train crawled along the green valleys. As we were coming down the Delaware towards Callicoon, where the Franciscans had their seminary, the sky had clouded over. We were slowing down, and the first houses of the village were beginning to file past on the road beside the track. A boy who had been swimming in the river came running up a path through the long grass, from the face of the thunderstorm that was just about to break. His mother was calling to him from the porch of one of the houses.
>
> I became vaguely aware of my own homelessness.
>
> When we had gone round the bend and I could see the tower of the seminary on the hilltop among the trees, I thought: I will never live in you: it is finished.[40]

Finished it was. He told all and was asked to withdraw his application. He left the seminary desolate, and stumbled into the nearest church to the confessional. There, kneeling — in his confusion — he blurted out a mixed up story of rejection to 'a thin bearded priest' who when Merton began to sob told him that he 'certainly did not belong in the monastery, still less the priesthood . . .' As he left the confessional he writes that he was 'completely broken in pieces'.[41]

Once again Merton had tasted the bitterness of rejection. But his natural courage and extraordinary spiritual energy came to the rescue, and paradoxically his commitment to live a disciplined religious life — now as a Franciscan tertiary was only strengthened.

> 'There could be no more question of living just like everyone else in the world. There could be no more compromises with the life that tried, at every turn, to feed me poison. I had to turn my back on these things.'[42]

He got a job teaching English at a Catholic College which suited him well. Slowly there was some healing. He was an excellent and lively teacher, he was writing a lot himself, and he loved his students. Privately however, he was constantly engaged in a battle within himself between the old and the new Thomas Merton that was struggling to come to birth.

War of a different scale constantly threatened too. By now it was 1940 and he faced the possibility of the draft. He had resolved to be a non-combatant. Eventually he was called to a medical and it was the poor state of the health of his teeth that saved him.

Gethsemani

And then quite suddenly the dramatic change came, the chance to finally leave 'Egypt'. Following his friend Dan Walsh's advice he had applied to spend Holy Week of 1941 at the Abbey of our Lady, Gethsemani, the Trappist

monastery in Kentucky. Writing as a monk from the monastery in 1947, he remembers vividly the details of his first
journey there. Arriving on the train at the little town of
Bardstown, he managed to get a lift to the monastery:

> I looked at the rolling country, and at the pale ribbon
> of road in front of us, stretching out as grey as lead in
> the light of the moon. Then suddenly I saw a steeple
> that shone like silver in the moonlight, growing into sight
> from behind a rounded knoll. The tires sang on the
> empty road, and, breathless, I looked at the monastery
> that was revealed before me as we came over the rise.
> At the end of an avenue of trees was a big rectangular
> block of buildings, all dark, with a church crowned by
> a tower and a steeple and a cross: and the steeple was
> as bright as platinum and the whole place was as quiet
> as midnight and lost in the all-absorbing silence and
> solitude of the fields. Behind the monastery was a dark
> curtain of woods, and over to the west was a wooded
> valley, and beyond that a rampart of wooded hills, a
> barrier and a defence against the world.
>
> And over all the valley smiled the mild, gentle Easter
> moon, the full moon in her kindness, loving this silent
> place.[43]

He goes on to describe with his extraordinary vividness
and eye for detail the awesome mystery and secret beauty
of this monastery full of silent praying men. In his enthusiasm, using language of romantic excess he describes it as
'the court of the Queen of Heaven . . . the centre of all the
vitality that is in America'.[44]

Above all it meant for him the end of this world — and
the possibility of a new one. At one point during his retreat
he describes seeing in the Church a young postulant 'in
dungarees' standing amidst the monks in their graceful
white cowls:

> 'For a couple of days it was that way. Practically the
> first thing you noticed when you looked at the choir, was

this young man in secular clothes, among all the monks. Then suddenly we saw him no more. He was in white. They had given him an oblate's habit, and you could not pick him out from the rest. The waters had closed over his head, and he was submerged in the community. He was lost. The world would hear of him no more. He had drowned to our society and had become a Cistercian.'[45]

At the end of the retreat he returned to his life of teaching, not daring after his earlier rejection to voice the hope that he too could be a monk.

In August 1941 he was challenged in his search from another direction: he ran into Catherine de Hueck who ran Friendship House in downtown Harlem and she challenged him to come and live there. While still clinging to his desire to be a Trappist he said yes, and during the first few weeks there his eyes were opened wide to the conditions of negroes in pre-Martin Luther-King America. He was appalled by their situation, and much moved by the faith of some Negro women whom he came to know, who emitted a sense 'of peace, of conquest'[46] in the midst of the cauldron of Harlem. Whilst it became clear that it was not his vocation to stay there, seeds were sown: later he was to be much involved in the struggle for Civil Rights in the 1960s.

Lost to the World

It was while he was still committed to going to Harlem that the crisis came of needing to resolve once and for all the agonising question as to whether or not he could be a Trappist. Eventually in the darkness of one night he found himself in the garden of the college in a kind of profound anguish and restlessness. He kneels before a shrine and pleads for a sense of direction:

Suddenly as soon as I had made that prayer, I became aware of the wood, the trees, the dark hills, the wet night wind, and then clearer than any of these obvious realities, in my imagination, I started to hear the great bell of Gethsemani ringing in the night — the bell in the big grey tower, ringing and ringing, as if it were just behind the first hill . . . The bell seemed to be telling me where I belonged — as if it were calling me home.[47]

The sense of knowing in the depths of his lonely soul that the Gethsemani which he had visited at Holy Week was truly his home overwhelmed him, and gave him the courage to risk rejection again. He rushed indoors and asked again if he could be a priest, and this time he was told by one of the senior friars there was no reason why not:

Father Philotheus had only one question: 'Are you sure you want to be a *Trappist*?' he asked me. 'Father', I answered, 'I want to give God everything.'[48]

Events moved rapidly. By the beginning of Advent having given away almost everything, he was ready to go, to leave St Bonaventure's and New York and the world, for Gethsemani. Reading it again one is reminded of the flight from Egypt, the haste of the Passover:

My train was in the evening . . . Where are you going Prof? said somebody as I passed out of the building . . . the cab door slammed . . . I did not turn to see the collection of heads that watched the parting cab . . . When we got to town there was still time for me to go to the church of . . . Then the Buffalo train came in through the freezing sleety rain, and I got on, and my last tie with the world I had known snapped and broke.[49]

On the 10th December 1941, Thomas Merton entered the monastery of Our Lady of Gethsemani, Kentucky. He had passed over — and as he saw it then, died to the world, and entered the 'court of the Queen of Heaven' — his Promised Land.

Reflection

It's a dramatic story, and at first sight rather strange and even alien. It is not many of us who enter a Trappist monastery, or who are cruelly orphaned as children. This may make the story seem remote: a painful story, a beautiful story too, and certainly powerfully written, but remote from the very ordinary and everyday struggles of most of us.

However, I suspect that despite the sharp outward differences, Merton's story as he told it in *The Seven Story Mountain* finds echoes in the early experiences of very many people who come to faith, and that is the book's enduring power.

Contrast and Change

The clearest theme of the autobiography is the theme of contrast and change. Again and again Merton contrasts the evil, darkness and chaos of the life of 'the world' — a world at his time plunging into war — with the light and beauty and order of Christ, and as he saw it then the Catholic Church. The contrast was focused sharply in his own soul and much of his perception of the world outside was a projection of the battle that raged within — something he clearly recognised later. He was a man in flight, in the end desperate and longing to get away from himself and his own appetites and find the peace of God. The place where he believed that would happen was within the strict structure and silence of Gethsemani. On entering the monastery he believed he had passed from death to life, his ties with the world had 'snapped and broke'. In the image he used of another young novice, he had 'drowned to the world and become a Cistercian' and so had stopped compromising with the life that had fed him 'poison'.

Throughout the book we are offered images of the sharpest contrast. At first sight what could be more in tune with the message of the Bible? The New Testament particularly is shot through with this theme of contrast and dramatic change. In its pages the darkness of 'the world' is turned

to light, death to life, sadness to joy, hope to despair,
disease to health, blindness to sight and deafness to hear-
ing. In the letters of Paul and the Gospel of John especially,
'the world', though the object of the love of God, is repeatedly seen in negative terms in contrast to life 'in Christ',
and it is Satan who is the prince of this world (John 14:30).
We are not to conform to this world (Rom 12:2) and the
world hates Christ for he 'gives evidence that its ways are
evil' (John 7:7). 'The world' similarly will hate the disciples
because they will not belong to the world (John 17:14).
Deliverance or rescue then from the 'present wicked world'
(Gal 1:14) is the very essence of salvation. In the ministry
of Jesus this deliverance from the powers of 'the world' is
focused in the lives of specific individuals: Legion is
restored to sanity, Bartimaeus sees again, Jairus's daughter
is raised to life, a possessed child is set free, a woman of
the streets is restored to the community and weeps over
his feet with joyful gratitude, a man with a withered hand
is healed, a paralytic walks . . . and so on.

Such contrast and dramatic change are offered as more
than a hope — they are the reality of a new life in God.
Through story, miracle, parable, and metaphor drawn
from the Gospels, the Acts of the Apostles and the Letters,
the message is of radical change in the lives of individuals
and whole communities. Faith in Christ it seems will bring
this about. An understanding of reality in terms of life 'in
Christ' or death in 'the world' is on offer here in terms of
clear cut contrast, and a choice is required. 'See I set before
you life or death, blessing or curse . . . choose life then so
that you may live . . .'(Deut 13:19). Such is the attraction
of evangelical faith simply presented. Merton's story resonates with this same contrasting theme.

I remember quite clearly understanding and grasping
faith in these terms of sharp contrast at the time of my
own 'conversion' at Oxford during the Spring term of 1968.
In the previous Autumn term there had been a 'mission'
to the University organised by the Christian Union. I was
away at the time struggling with exams, but on returning
I remember how disconcerting it was to find that some of

the closest friends I had made had become religious and were constantly rushing off to Bible studies and even worse, prayer meetings. There was a certain kind of jaunty confidence in their manner, and it wasn't long before I too, rebelliously I remember smoking cigarettes, attended my first Bible study. After a good deal of arguing and late night hot-house discussion, I too fell prey to the confident certainties of evangelical religion. Quietly helped one night by the presence of a good and gentle friend, and kneeling childlike beside the small bed in my tiny room in St Aldate's, I opened my heart to God as best I knew how. The effect was entirely undramatic, and yet I was conscious, and so were those around me, that a barrier had been crossed and I was now 'converted'.

Much of the attraction to someone as insecure as I undoubtedly was, was the simplicity of the clear structure of belief that was offered and the sense of direction and purpose that this new faith gave with the comfort of close-knit belonging in what we termed the 'fellowship'. Within this structure of belief the world was instantly clarified in terms of certain fundamental simplicities, marked by contrast. The Bible was the infallible word of God in contrast to all other literature; the world and I as part of it was 'fallen', blackened by sin and evil, in contrast to God's total goodness and so there was a profound separation; there was an offer of free forgiveness in Christ who had died as my substitute; there was a promise of a changed life with Christ as Lord in contrast to all that had gone before; the Church was the community of those who had been 'saved' in contrast to the sinful world around . . . etc. Now looking back, it appears a pretty thin gruel and intellectually meagre too. Most of the difficult questions of faith and doubt were simply 'answered' by dogmatic assertion from the particular understanding of the Bible which was preached in the Christian Union and which was the basic plank of the whole structure. But this emphasis on 'the authority of the Bible' as it was preached, was part of the attraction! In a way it stopped you having to think, which would have simply added to a life already confused, and enabled faith to be presented as an authoritative whole. As long as you believed in it, the whole system was water-tight. For the time being such certainty was reassuring and it was only later while at theological college that the structure began to leak, and eventually sank. But at the time, the emotional satisfaction of belonging, belonging in the community of faith, belonging to God and finding a clear sense of direction, outweighed any intellectual doubts that may have been lurking. I do remember though being quite thrown one day by a good-natured taunt from a Jewish friend who asked me, as I claimed to literally believe every word of the Bible, did I really believe that Joshua made the sun stand still? (Josh 10:13). Of course I did, I confidently retorted, and then wondered, did I? On Sundays we packed the little church behind St Aldate's which we saw as the truly 'sound' evangelical church in the town and then went out — convictions reaffirmed — to 'evangelise' our acquaintances in the world of the University outside.

While I came later to question every one of the simple certainties that I had swallowed whole, nevertheless this kind of experience, repeated in different guise in the stories of many others, needs to be seen as a common first stage of religious experience. Driven by a sense of insecurity, emotional need, and in the case of Merton a profound homelessness in the world, it is a grasping and idealising of an authoritarian structure of belief which offers a superficial order in the midst of a chaos of emotional complexity. In my case this structure took the form of the arid and abstract propositions of a simple rational Protestantism. In Merton's infinitely more rich case, it was clad in the rich and mysterious adornment of pre-Vatican II Catholic splendour. In his case too, the faith he grasped so eagerly and threw himself into so totally was earthed and rooted in a rich intellectual tradition and was part of the soil of whole cultures. In his visit to Cuba in 1936, he was deeply moved by the natural religion of that society expressed one day at Mass at St Francis Church Havana, when he watched a group of children clustered round the altar chanting the opening words of the Creed in Spanish . . . 'Creo en Dios . . .' As he watched and heard the children he writes of a vivid awareness . . . the light of God's presence . . . 'a light . . . so bright . . . so profound . . . so intimate . . . and yet this light was in a certain sense *ordinary*'.[50] Here was a religion bursting forth in the innocent voices of children that was part of the very roots and fabric of that Latin society. He had been similarly moved by the signs of the religion of mediaeval Catholic Europe that he had glimpsed as a child himself in St Antonin, and in the other small towns of southern France.

A New Creation ?

Whatever the difference is between this kind of rich arrival in faith, and my own experience and the experiences of many others who have made a sudden grasp at faith though in much poorer forms, I suspect that the psychological and spiritual mechanism is fundamentally the same. There is an eager embracing of the things of God which are for order, and a struggle to leave, to put behind and even to despise 'the world', the realm of chaos. There is a heartfelt plea for a new and instant creation in all the simplicity and immediacy of the Genesis account: over the swirling chaos of darkness and nothingness God said 'Let there be light', and — there was light! The promise is believed that in the passing into the Kingdom of the beloved Son there will be wrought some kind of miraculous transformation. Somehow in our simplicity we expect the whole world to be different. Towards the end of the book Merton writes of how he prepared his younger brother John Paul who had visited the Monastery for baptism. There is something touching about the two orphaned brothers grasping hold of the simple and immediate promise of grace — a grace that will surely instantly transform everything:

'Once you have grace,' I said to him, 'you are free . . . When you are baptised there is no power in existence that can force you to commit a sin — nothing that will

be able to drive you to it against your own conscience.
And if you merely will it, you will be free for ever,
because the strength will be given you, as much as you
need, and as often as you ask, and as soon as you ask,
and generally long before you ask for it, too.'[51]

The factor perhaps most at play in this kind of conversion
experience is surely insecurity. Such conversion occurs
where there has been to use Paul Tillich's phrase, a profound 'shaking of the foundations', or very little foundations at all in terms of good self-esteem. Authoritarian
religion, like any authoritarian structure of secular belief,
offers a coherent framework eagerly grasped in particular
moments of vulnerability.

Inner Doubt

But such structure cannot in the long run substitute for
that good sense of self, painfully built over many years,
which is the foundation of health in any personality. However, it can mimic it, and mask problems that go on lurking,
unknowingly, below the surface — and that is its danger.
For a while all may indeed be transformed. The new con-
vert may believe that he or she is indeed 'ransomed, healed,
restored, forgiven'. All is light and sunshine in the Lord,
and the tenets of the new faith, whether Protestant, Catholic, Socialist, or anything else are vigorously and unquestionably believed and defended. But inner doubt, hollowness, or pain will persist, hidden but paradoxically revealed
by the iron conviction in the certainties of faith, and the
need — in Protestantism particularly — to constantly press
them on to others.

The *Seven Storey Mountain* is the colourful story of such a
clear-cut conversion. It is a rich story amplified and coloured by Merton's poetic imagination and use of words
and it touches heights and depths in all our lives. It is this
which makes it a modern classic. There is too towards the
end clear signs that he sensed that all was not well, that
despite the rigours of the Monastery and his best endeav-

ours he is still 'shadowed' by another self, another Thomas Merton — 'the old man of the sea'[52] — who will not leave him easily. He senses too that his vocation may be in a negative way, to explore as a way to God suffering and darkness. But nevertheless the overall impression of the book conveyed by his particular genius is contrast, and grace transforming. Despite the simplicities and idealising, it is hard not to be moved by what Gethsemani meant for him and what such a place often symbolises for us:

> The soul of the monk is a Bethlehem where Christ comes to be born ... the Advent liturgy prepares that Bethlehem with songs and canticles of ardent desire.
>
> It is a desire all the more powerful, in the spiritual order, because the world around you is dead. Life has ebbed to its dregs. The trees are stripped bare. The birds forget to sing. The grass is brown and grey. You go out to the fields with mattocks to dig up the briars. The sun gives its light, as it were, in faint intermittent explosions ...
>
> But the cold stones of the Abbey Church ring with a chant that glows with living flame, with clean, profound desire. It is an austere warmth, the warmth of Gregorian chant. It is deep beyond ordinary emotion, and that is one reason why you never get tired of it. It never wears you out by making a lot of cheap demands on your sensibilities. Instead of drawing you out into the open field of feelings where your enemies, the devil and your own imagination and the inherent vulgarity of your own corrupted nature can get at you with their blades and cut you to pieces, it draws you within, where you are lulled in peace and recollection and where you find God.
>
> You rest in Him, and He heals you with His secret wisdom.[53]

This sense of getting lost and hiding — childlike — within the embrace and clear limits of a faith structure that is authoritative and given, is and has been a beginning point in the personal search for the Kingdom in the lives of countless converts. It is I suppose a kind of womb experience, reminding us of St John's image of the second birth. Of course some structures are more rooted in the reality of God's truth than others. This is true I think of Merton's rich and earthed Catholicism over against the kind of abstract Protestantism which I embraced. Perhaps the particular weakness of evangelical Protestantism is its rational and abstract nature. The danger is that it offers people more of a mental straightjacket to be escaped from, than a womb for the birth of a whole person into the world. And yet oddly this can also be its very attraction. It can surely at least be seen as an authentic, if flawed, beginning point.

Of course it needs to be said that beginning in faith is not always like this. There are very many others who have less need for such certainties and for dramatic change. For them growth and faith is from the beginning far more gradual and punctuated with uneasy questions and nagging doubt. Many come to faith maintaining and sustaining a healthy, vigorous and critical intellectual questioning even while they recognise that faith demands at some point a surrender of the heart and will. Their fundamental insight from the beginning is that faith is a long and hard journey, and there are few instant answers which last. And there are others quite simply who have been nurtured in what feels like an authentic faith from childhood, and will say they have never known what it means not to believe.

At this point it is worth pausing for a moment and reflecting — if you see yourself as a Christian — on your own faith beginnings. It may be said that the deepest truth is that for very many, faith has its real beginnings in the earliest experiences of infancy and on that we shall touch in the next section. But that notwithstanding, looking back most of us can point to particular moments and people in our story, where we crossed some barrier, despite our doubts said yes . . . or less consciously were simply moved forward by something beyond ourselves. We need to recognise our own turning points or staging posts in faith though we may have to search for them hidden in the undergrowth of our past. They are moments when we were particularly conscious of change.

This is the importance of the Passover for the Jews. In this event they remember. They left Egypt and crossed the waters and journeyed into the desert. It appears from their very early grumbling against Moses soon after they were free, that they too had expected some kind of instant comfort and promised land, and had not reckoned on the hard rigours of the long search ahead. Their story offers the ultimate paradigm of faith, a paradigm made vividly personal in the story of Thomas Merton. He fled to the Monastery out of the world. He embraced the security of the Order and the structure of life at Gethsemani. He came home. But it was not long before he entered a desert of the spirit and this is where we come to the second phase of the personal search, the point perhaps where the search really begins.

Chapter 5: The Ruins of my Heart

A Forbidding Fortress

To enter a Trappist Monastery in the early 1940s meant a complete break with the outside world.[1] It was a dramatic, radical and total severing of living contact with any active participation in the life of society. The rule was clear: having entered the Order the monk would never leave the monastery except for essential visits to the nearby town. Contact by post with the outside world was also strictly limited — just four letters a year, and all mail was strictly censored.

Merton of course knew this when he was formally admitted as a postulant on 13th December 1941. It was the very essence of why he was going there. He had resolved to leave the world, 'to be lost to all created things, to die to them and to the knowledge of them . . .'[2] The monastery was as near human society could come to his ideal. 'The aim of all human activity was to be the recovery of Eden and it was the nature of Eden to be unchangeable'[3] declared Hugh of St Victor in the twelfth century, and in 1941 Gethsemani was unquestionably Merton's Eden, his ideal, his paradise.

Not only was it a severing of contact with the life of twentieth century America, it meant a step back in time into an austere and stark way of life that had changed scarcely at all since the Middle Ages. It is hard for the layman to grasp the extent of this austerity. 'Arduous, confined, raw'[4] is how Mott describes their daily life which began at 2 a.m. when they were woken in their tiny cubicles to say the Night Office. The rest of the night was spent in prayer, meditation and holy reading in the great church which was as cold as a tomb in winter. The day involved a succession of Offices beginning with Prime at 5.30 a.m., going on to the climax of the day, High Mass, at 7.45, and ending with the Angelus at 6.10 before retiring to bed at 7 p.m. Constant prayer and meditation was interspersed with very simple meals and hard manual work. For clothing, the monks dressed in coarse white wool garments and wore strange mediaeval underwear, the same in winter as summer. Dwelling on the Exodus theme, Merton wrote of this white cowl given after first vows as 'the garment of contemplation that envelopes and encloses the body in its ample folds like the cloud that protected the Children of Israel in their escape through the desert'.[5]

A particular feature of Trappist life which focused their penitential vocation was carried out in 'the Chapter of Faults'. A whole range of humiliations for small misdeeds could be meted out although the ritual nature to some extent removed the sting of personal pain.[6] It was all part of the understanding of penance that was at the heart of the original Trappist vocation.

To the outsider this harsh and severe life with its sparse diet, total silence, hard work, demanding religion and physical confinement, may appear repellent and even unhealthy. And yet its authoritative structure, the simple beauty of worship, and its total sacrifice captured the heart of the young postulant. For him Gethsemani was the place that was at last his home.

In fact, when he joined the Order, despite the rule and his best intentions, Merton had by no means left 'the world'. Though he did not venture out for seven years, and after that only occasionally until his last journey to the East in 1968, almost from the first days, he was engaged in writing. He himself was very ambivalent about this, his 'second vocation'. But his Superiors recognised his gift, and also the need for literature about Cistercian life, and he was soon showered with requests. The result was that an eextraordinary flood of writing developed, and through his journals we are let into the progress of his silent journey.

It is necessary to pause here. If his embracing of Christianity and his subsequent flight from the world to this

Eden and his ordination to the priesthood marked a first phase — a first conversion — then the crisis in the desert experience at the beginning of the 1950s suggests a second phase. Though everything seemed to be disintegrating, it was in fact the beginning of a far deeper movement. In this period Merton entered into the heart of his vocation.

However, before we try to understand this crisis as fully as possible on the basis of his own writings, it is important to set the scene, the personal context of this journey. We need to try to grasp something of what Gethsemani in this early Edenic period meant to him. Why and how did it so deeply appeal?

The first and most obvious appeal was in the *security* it offered. The Abbey of Our Lady of Gethsemani in the hills of Kentucky, is a massive solid structure founded by French monks in 1848.[7] The sheer solidity and permanence of the buildings spoke of a permanence that had been entirely lacking in Merton's life from the beginning. Within those huge thick walls, the detailed structure of Cistercian life, the dogmatic nature of pre-Vatican II Catholicism, and the rigid understanding of authority combined to offer an austere but rigid framework that was deeply attractive to him. But more than that, it offered him immediately a way out of himself to God in worship. It was his dream come true. He writes of his first evening: 'When we began to change the Magnificat I almost wept . . . with thanksgiving and happiness as I croaked the words in my dry, hoarse throat . . . I was really there at last, really in the monastery, and chanting God's liturgy with his monks.'[8] At this stage he was a postulant. Later, in 1947 he took solemn vows. There remains throughout this early writing a child-like quality in his journal which bears testimony to the depth of his need for this, his first real home and family. One of the vows was a vow of 'stability', a vow to remain part of Gethsemani forever. It was a vow which later he was to struggle with, but on the day after his 'profession', he writes: 'I am left with a deep sense of union with all the other monks . . . I am part of Gethsemani. I belong to the family.' He describes 'a deep and warm realisation' of

being 'immersed in my community'.[9] Later when a group
of Brothers leave to found a new house in Utah he writes
of the pain of their departure: 'We will miss them very
much.'[10] The family had a very hierarchical authority structure, and Merton underlines the importance of the vow of
obedience to 'Father Abbot': . . . 'It is best,' he solemnly
wrote, 'to take religious obedience quite literally . . .'[11] Finally, there is something delightfully childlike about his first
excursion out of the Monastery after seven years to act as
interpreter for the Vicar-General (who only spoke French)
on a visit to a nearby convent.

So he told them, in French, to love their vocations, and
I translated his message into English. I think they were
happy. One sister held the black hat I had been wearing
in her hand while I drank a glass of ginger ale and ate
a cookie, and was too shy to look at any of the sisters.[12]

Some contrast with the womanising undergraduate of
Cambridge days!

If the life offered this all-embracing and much needed
security, the building itself set in 700 acres of beautiful and
remote woods and fields seems to settle and heal him. Place
had always been important for him. On the last page of
The Seven Storey Mountain he had listed the staging posts on
his journey to Gethsemani: Prades, Bermuda, St Antonin,
Oakham, London, Cambridge, Rome, New York, Columbia, Corpus Christi, St Bonaventure.[13] In the journal he
writes lovingly of this new permanent home: 'It is important to know where you are put, on the face of the earth.
Physically, the monastery is in great solitude . . . One or
two houses a mile and a half away and then woods and
pastures and bottoms and cornfields and hills for miles and
miles.'[14] The journal goes on to be illumined with startling
descriptions of this rich natural solitude. It is more than
just a delight in the natural world. All he sees around
him become the very mediators of God's presence. 'How
necessary it is,' he writes, 'for monks to work in the fields,
in the rain, in the sun, in the mud, in the clay, in the wind:

these are our spiritual directors and our novice-masters.'[15] In Merton's eyes every natural detail, the breeze on the pond, the hawk in flight, the tall summer corncrests nodding in the wind, heavy snowflakes vanishing at the touch of the warm earth on the first day of Spring, the meadowlarks feeding and singing in the wet grass . . . every detail is 'charged with the reality and presence of God'.[16] This sense of the life of God speaking through the natural world is heightened by the monastic life itself. The silence and the hard manual work kept the monks close to the natural rhythms and there is an absence of the external racket of cars, television sets, radios — just the occasional train whistling in the valley. In the June of 1949, still in the apparently blissful early womblike period soon after his ordination, he writes of sitting on a high bank looking out over part of the monastery grounds:

> Right under me was a dry creak, with clean pools lying like glass between the shale pavements of the stream, and the shale was as white and crumpled as sea-biscuit. Down in the glen were the songs of marvellous birds. I saw the gold-orange flame of an Oriole in a tree . . . There was a cardinal whistling . . . the best song was that of two birds that sounded as wonderful as nightingales and their song echoed through the wood . . . The echo made the place sound more remote, and self-contained, more perfectly enclosed, and more like Eden.[17]

This appreciation of the natural world, birds, trees, cornfields, rain (Merton loved rain), and the silence of the woods, was not just confined to this Eden period. It remained with him, and particularly when he moved to the Hermitage in the mid–60s, deepening his suspicion of urbanised technological culture. He sensed that our sanity and our survival are intimately tied up with knowing our place as part of the natural world. To convey something of this contemplative sense of the life of God in the natural world, two pieces from this later period taken from *Conjectures of a Guilty Bystander*:

How the valley awakes. At two-fifteen in the morning there are no sounds except in the monastery: the bells ring, the Office begins. Outside, nothing, except perhaps a bullfrog saying 'Om' in the creek or in the guesthouse pond. Some nights he is in Samadhi; there is not even 'Om'. The mysterious and uninterrupted whooping of the whippoorwill begins about three, these mornings. He is not always near. Sometimes there are two whooping together, perhaps a mile away in the woods in the east.

The first chirps of the waking day birds mark the *'point vierge'* of the dawn under a sky as yet without real light, a moment of awe and inexpressible innocence, when the Father in perfect silence opens their eyes. They begin to speak to Him, not with fluent song, but with an awakening question that is their dawn state at the *'point vierge'*. Their condition asks if it is time for them to 'be'. He answers 'yes'. Then, they one by one wake up, and become birds. They manifest themselves as birds, beginning to sing. Presently they will be fully themselves, and will even fly.

Meanwhile, the most wonderful moment of the day is that when creation in its innocence asks permission to 'be' once again, as it did on the first morning that ever was.[18]

Secondly, one Easter morning after the suffocating rituals of High Mass:

The less said about the Easter morning Pontifical Mass the better. Interminable pontifical manoeuverings, with the 'Master of Ceremonies' calling every play, and trying to marshal the ministers into formation and keep things moving. Purple zuchetto and cappa magna and of course it had to be our Mexican novice who was appointed to carry the long train (this inwardly made me furious and practically choked any desire I may have had to sing alleluias). The church was stifling with solemn, feudal, and unbreathable fictions. This taste for plush, for ornamentation, for display strikes me as secular, no matter how much it is supposed to be 'for the glory of God'. The spring outside seemed much more sacred. Easter afternoon I went to the lake and sat in silence looking at the green buds, the wind skimming the utterly silent surface of the water, a muskrat slowly paddling to the other side. Peace and meaning. Sweet spring air. One could breathe. The alleluias came back by themselves.[19]

The security of the life focused in worship, and the silence and remoteness of this natural Eden were two important strands in the appeal of Gethsemani. But the dominant note that comes across is the very *austerity* of the life itself. He had joined the Cistercians *of the Strict Observance*, a break-away Order from the main Cistercians, formed in the seventeenth century under a far more rigorous rule established by Abbot de Rancé at his Abbey of La Trappe. Merton's nature was always to go the whole way. There could be no compromise. The Franciscan Father had pressed him on the night when he felt his vocation was in the balance, 'Are you sure you want to be a Trappist?' 'Father,' came the reply, 'I want to give God *everything*.' The renunciation of the 'world' had to be total. In his struggle with himself, the break had to be complete. It seems that only that forbidding fortress of God lost in the silence of the hills would do.

As well as the clear need for a total offering and sacrifice, there may have been something deeply positive at work here also that was to bear rich fruit later and is at the heart of this second conversion. It is clear that from the first visit, the profound silence and austerity of the Trappists, and the physical solitude of Gethsemani itself, touched and resonated with hidden depths within his own soul. Here was a place where a man could enter into a solitude that was quite impossible in the life of 'the world' or in the life of more active Orders. From the beginning Merton sensed he needed this solitude, needed to explore the darkness and emptiness of life without dependence on any mortal thing or person, needed to find God in the darkness of his own loneliness and emptiness. Here was the fearful but hopeful attraction of the Trappist life. Was there awakening in him, buried and painful memories of another unasked for loneliness? Once a cavern of emptiness had been torn open in his own soul. Buried in him was there the hidden question: could God be found there?

The search for greater solitude was to become the key orientation of his life, only partially satisfied in the mid-60s when he was given permission to live in the Hermitage in the woods. Throughout the 1950s he searched for a way into deeper solitude and even considered leaving Gethsemani for one of the Orders which focused on the hermit life. And yet though frustrated in his search, he was faithful to his vow of stability. It seems he was also nervous of such solitude, knowing perhaps that it could drive a man mad, and even at one stage in the mid-50s he consciously refused the opportunity of the Hermitage when it was offered by the Abbot, believing that he was not yet ready for it.

But all this was to come. Initially, secure in the womb of this new home and despite a certain fragility and the occasional outburst of lingering self-disgust, he was happy. And the happiness appeared to last right up to his ordination to the priesthood in the summer of 1949. It was an important date and he writes of being deeply affected by it: 'My priestly ordination was, the one great secret for which I had been born.'[20] As he says his first Masses, he writes of standing at the altar 'with my eyes all washed in the light that is eternity' and becoming 'agelessly reborn'.[21] Later he writes of becoming 'Somebody Else . . . raised to a higher and much simpler and cleaner level of being'.[22] It is the climax of his early period. Truly he had arrived and was now secure enough to face the desert of the spirit, that second conversion, where a new Thomas Merton would be born.

'The Self that begins is not the Self that arrives'

James Finlay in his book *Merton's Palace of Nowhere* writes: 'Merton leads us along a journey to God in which the self that begins the journey is not the self that arrives. The self that begins is the self that we thought ourselves to be. It is this self that dies along the way . . .'[23] Growth in the life of the Spirit, he suggests, is not one steady process of spiritual enlightenment, but marked by pain and darkness before hope comes, disintegration before the gift of the new, death before resurrection. Usually there are many crises before the new self is sufficiently formed. This was certainly true of Merton himself. Throughout the 'suffering 50s' he was to undergo many crises of the spirit before the new man emerged in the 60s to 'choose the world'[24] that he had so determinedly rejected in the 40s. But the most acute crisis appears to be the first during the eighteen months following his ordination in the summer of 1949. In his journal he described it as an 'abysmal testing' and 'a disintegration of my spirit'.[25] We may ask, what led to it? Undoubtedly a strong contributory factor must have been the physical hardship and pressure of the way of life: the unremitting hard work, very poor diet and little sleep that he endured month after month, year after year. For all its emphasis on silence and contemplation the monastery was a hive of activity, and on one occasion he writes: 'I have fallen into the great indignity I have written against — I am a contemplative who is ready to collapse from overwork.'[26] And yet was it only the pressure and suffocating regime of this busy monastery?

Reading the journal, one senses that deeper forces were at work here leading Merton into a crisis and desert of the spirit that is both full of terror and yet paradoxically a place of hope. References to this crisis are scattered throughout the period from the autumn of 1949 to December 1950, and yet it occurred in the midst of normality. He was able to share in the normal monastic life although occasionally the fear overwhelms him and he finds himself struggling with the simplest tasks. This experience of spiritual torment and upheaval in the midst of normality is a common experience of many who undergo the kind of disintegration and re-making that Merton recounts. It is remarkable how even while a fundamental re-creation is going on, people find the resources to carry on with at least a facade of normal life. Merton describes his own 'disintegration' as 'a slow submarine earthquake . . .' In which he felt 'summoned to battle with joy and with fear . . .'[27] He sensed that something new was happening within which he did not understand and yet was of supreme importance. Briefly through scattered entries we can trace this desert journey and perhaps appreciate something of the feeling of it through his words.

A Desert of the Spirit

In September 1949 after the ordination he writes of being 'unutterably alone' in the midst of all living things and of a self that defiles everything if it attempts to give itself away.[28] He speaks of being alone because he is 'nothing';[29] of an interior fighting and of a power that 'keeps seizing my heart in its fist and wringing cries out of me . . .'; in the same entry he refers to his soul 'cringeing and doubling up and subconsciously getting ready for the next tidal wave . . . all I had left in my heart was an abyss of self-hatred, waiting for the next appalling sea.'[30] In December on the anniversary of his eight years in Gethsemani he speaks of feeling 'less clean that I did when I thought I was throwing my civil identity away.'[31] Echoing a sense of infancy, he writes on the 15th December of working in the woods in the afternoon feeling 'lonely and small and humiliated — chopping down dead trees with a feeling that perhaps I was not even a real person any more . . . feeling of fear, dejection, non-existence.'[32] On the Vigil of St Thomas (20th December), and significantly the very mid-point of winter, the eve of the day of greatest darkness, he writes of standing in the church being stripped of every illusion about himself, his reading, his writing, his enthusiasms. In the next entry he speaks bluntly of the death of Thomas Merton: 'They can have Thomas Merton. He's dead. Father Louis (his monastic name) — he's half-dead too.'[33] More and more he is searching out the total solitude, a kind of non-existence — no dependence on anything.

He describes poignantly the Traxcavator pulling down the remains of the old horse barn that is half in ruins. He writes: 'It is fear that is driving me into solitude . . . I am exhausted by fear.'[34] He finds himself hanging on to the lines of Psalm 54 and writes of the strength of the liturgy: 'My heart is troubled within me and the fear of death is falling upon me.' On the 30th December he writes of 'the dead rot of acedia that eats out your substance with discouragement and fear . . .'[35] and he adds harshly 'it makes you wish you could get something respectable, with a real pain attached to it, like cancer or a tumour on the brain.'[36]

What are we to make of this? It is a harsh wilderness experience. He is led to a place of nothingness and over-whelmed by fear and death — but it leads to a spiritual re-birth. It is important to ask what is happening? Can we understand, at least in part, the process of this strange spiritual agony?

The tradition of psychoanalytic thought would ask what, within his new security, is being re-lived here, being re-owned, re-experienced? When else in his life had he known such feelings . . . loneliness, smallness, humiliation, fear, dejection, non-existence? It is of course impossible defini-tively to answer these questions, and Merton himself doesn't pose them. And yet even as we read these entries it is hard not to be reminded of the account of the death of his parents experienced at so young an age. When he heard the news that his mother was about to die, conveyed to him by a letter, which indicated she would never see him again he writes of 'a tremendous weight of sadness and depression' settling on him. 'It was not the grief of a child with pangs of sorrow and many tears. It had some-thing of the heavy complexity and gloom of adult grief . . .'[37] He was just six years old. In the autobiography the whole event is passed over quickly, and strangely never mentioned again. Nine years later he heard by phone the news that his father was dying and he recalls sitting there 'in the dark, unhappy room . . . with all the innumerable elements of my isolation crowding in upon me from every side . . .'[38] Following on this he developed what appears a rather distant relationship with his guardian Tom Bennett. There was the humiliating interview about his chaotic life at Cambridge, and the rejection of being told not to return. A few years later he was to lose both grandparents, and so become an orphan. It is a harrowing bombardment of loss and rejection. In the loss of his parents particularly it would seem that he experienced a degree of pain that would have been too much to bear and be absorbed at his young age. Such pain however does not just melt away. It lies buried within. As we have seen, he was remarkably resilient. Out of this emotional carnage an adult self emerged who was garrulous, accomplished, intellectual, enormously colourful and attractive, and yet on his own admission — profoundly insecure. So he searched for a new home and in the monastery he found it and reached for the embrace of God. God we may say, took him and within the security of his vocation led him again into the valley of the shadow of death and non-being. Once again and over a long time he entered into an experience of emptiness and fear, loneliness, humiliation and smallness, there to discover in these darkest places a source of life and light that was pure gift. It led to the gift of a new self.

He writes that December 1950 was a turning point. After the 'abysmal testing' he writes of discovering 'a spring of new life, and a peace and a happiness that I had never known before and which subsisted in the face of nameless, interior terror.' And then he adds significantly: 'And now, for the first time, I began to know what it means to be *alone*.'[39]

In this last stage of *the Sign of Jonas* he refers repeatedly to a sense of growth and change and new identity in God. April 1951: 'My road has taken a new turning. It seems to me that I have been asleep for nine years and before that I was dead.'[40] 13th June: 'I have become very different from what I used to be. The man who began this journal is dead just as the man who finished *The Seven Storey Mountain* when this journal began was also dead, and what is more the man who was the central figure in *The Seven*

Storey Mountain was dead over and over . . . *The Seven Storey Mountain* is the work of a man I never even heard of . . .' and he goes on with wry humour 'and this journal is getting to be the production of somebody to whom I never had the dishonour of an introduction.'[41] Later in the same entry in his new role as 'Master of the Scholastics' he writes: 'Thus I stand on the threshold of a new existence . . . It is as if I were beginning all over again to be a Cistercian.' He is moving beyond 'monastic adolescence . . . with no time for anything but the essentials. The only essential is not an idea or', he adds significantly, 'an ideal: it is God Himself.'[42]

Perhaps the most notable change, a change of immense importance in Merton's later writing were the first signs of the end of the priggish world-denying streak in him that was so much a part of the autobiography. With the discovery of an inner integration previously unknown and so an end to the old self-dramatising Merton, the world which had acted as a mirror to this 'false self' simply no longer threatened. Now in the new era he writes with endearing humility for the first time and in an entirely new way about the world he had previously despised and fled from: he writes of the goodness of people, despite being enmeshed in the evils of war. His time in the Monastery has given him 'perspective'. Earlier in the same entry: 'I have come to the monastery to find my place in the world,' and further down he adds; 'My first duty is to start, for the first time, to live as a member of a human race which is no more (and no less) ridiculous than I am myself.'[43] Finally he writes of a new desert whose name is 'compassion . . . it is a solitude where God is with me . . . he sits in the ruins of my heart, preaching his gospel to the poor.'[44]

It was certainly not the case that in and through this one crisis the whole work of re-creation was done. There were to be other crises and bouts of nervous exhaustion through the 50s. But nevertheless it does seem that in this period some kind of radical shift and sea-change took place — a depth of healing which led to a re-orientation and a new direction that was to be permanent, and which he followed out of the suffering 50s into a third 'conversion' in the 60s — 'to choose the world'.

Reflection

In reflecting on this second phase of Merton's journey, let us summarise some fundamental themes: first, no instant miraculous transformation. 'Eden' is a place of fear as well as joy. Second, the importance of 'stability' in providing the necessary space and reassurance for inner struggle. Third, the 'disintegration' of the spirit comes unbidden. But beyond the disintegration he finds new resources and the beginning of a learning to live from another centre. Above all this 'second conversion' marks an intensifying of his need for solitude. It is *the* route for him, to God. On the last page of the autobiography he looks ahead to the pain and the possibility of this strange vocation:

> And when you have been praised a little and loved a little I will take away all your gifts and all your love and all your praise and you will be utterly forgotten and abandoned and you will be nothing, a dead thing, a rejection. And in that day you shall begin to possess the solitude you have so long desired. And your solitude will bear immense fruit in the souls of men you will never see on earth.[45]

Two Traditions of Soul Making

Where does such a need for such profound solitude come from in a man who was not going mad, indeed was one of the most deeply sane men of our time? Two imperatives suggest themselves. One, clearly his own self-understanding, was the impelling need to press forward into the darkness of the spiritual journey, into 'The Dark Night of the Soul' struggling to break free from the tainted self, and to learn in the darkness of pure faith, a kind of naked trust. The other, suggesting itself from his own account of his early life, is best put as a question: was there also a profound and intuitive need to visit again some forgotten place of deep emotional pain and suffering? It may be that both imperatives drawn from two separate but complimentary traditions of soul making are at work here: on the one hand the desert way of spirituality, and on the other, the tradition of psychoanalysis. We do not know. But Alan Jones' suggestion that we need to learn from both of them, is appropriate and helpful. For too long, he suggests, these two traditions have had very little to do with one another in the task of 'soul making'. We need to work with both, and see them as 'twins', spawned, he suggests, from the same parent, the desert.[46]

The first imperative, a need to deepen the search into the negative or 'apophatic' way of believing — the way of 'not knowing' — becomes a dominant theme in the later writings and is the route to Merton's 'Palace of Nowhere' — the 'true self' given in the darkness of pure faith.[47] We shall try to look more closely at this in the next section. But the second imperative — that we can understand in terms of psychotherapy — a need to revisit and reclaim a lost inner desert of the spirit blasted out in childhood, clearly presents itself, as we read the journal and reflect on the early years. Other than a laconic comment in the middle of the difficult period that 'in the natural order, perhaps solitaries are made by severe mothers',[48] Merton himself does not explicitly suggest any psychoanalytical understanding of his struggle. He simply refers to 'a sort of slow, submarine earthquake which produced strange commotions on the visible psychological surface of my life', and writes 'I have no way of explaining what it was.'[49] His loss of words should make us hesitant before suggesting too quickly what was going on here. And we cannot of course know. Nevertheless, as we read the account of him finding himself overwhelmed by inexplicable feelings of deep loneliness, dejection, fear, non-existence etc, in addition to the interpretation that this was all part of the experience of spiritual *acedia* (a not uncommon experience in the monastic life), it is hard not to make a connection with those traumatic and repeated experiences of bereavement and loss suffered at so young an age. Whether or not such a connection is accurate, we cannot tell. It simply presents itself. And for our purpose now, that question is not perhaps important. What *is* important is what the fragmentary account of his experience may suggest to us. What may we take from it for a better understanding of *our* search and journey?

First, it reminds us that Christian discipleship may not be the recipe for instant peace and joy that is sometimes claimed. In fact the reverse. His experience suggests that for some, at some point, psychological upheaval may well be a result of belonging to Christ. The pattern of his experience seems to have been that after his conversion and the difficult business of finding an Order, his first years in the monastery, as we have seen, were happy — even at times idyllic. That is often the case with new converts. But then after the ordination there comes this slow eruption into consciousness of nameless hidden fears. How can we make sense of this? What may be going on?

Giving God Everything

A clue suggests itself in the *way* Merton offered himself: 'I want to give God *everything*' he had said, and prayed, and meant it from the depths of his young heart. Perhaps that is precisely what, in his suffering, he is doing. Without consciously realising it or being able to control it as it occurred, he is giving God everything, his mind allowing up into consciousness the totality of his life's experience, the emerging from the submarine depths those things that for years had lain buried and hidden. It is a process of being purged. What we may see here is a picture of the implications of total Christian discipleship. God wants everything, and there is our need to give everything, share everything, and reveal everything. It is a need in all love relationships of any depth — provided that we can be sufficiently reassured that in the process of such revelation, we shall not be destroyed.

The tradition of psychoanalysis teaches that profound

individual pain and damage does not simply melt away with the passage of time but rather the wounds stubbornly remain and the mind acts like a forgetful squirrel burying and storing them. Those profoundly painful experiences from the early years which couldn't be sufficiently shared and felt at the time are buried in the subconscious while the innocent and ignorant conscious mind may believe that all darkness has been forgotten and passed away into history. But those kind of hidden memories remain, and continue to exercise a strange, pervasive and frequently disabling power. It is a disablement that in certain situations where memories are triggered can be acute, and profoundly damaging both to the individual concerned and to others. Then in addition to the buried wound or grief, there is the whole business of the defences needed against it. Energy is required to maintain mental barricades that can render the individual a virtual stranger to himself and drive him to the margins of the conscious mind. Further time and energy are spent devising obsessive strategies for survival. It can be an exhausting and costly business, and all for the purpose of self-protection against the emergence of bitter hurts that were simply too threatening and painful to bear at the time. We thus become engaged in a very elaborate cover-up job and it is a sad truth that the whole apparatus of religion with its emphasis upon behavioural control has frequently been hi-jacked into the task of maintaining it. People will live for years, for whole lifetimes in this kind of situation, and somehow succeed in surviving. We can become very adept at managing ourselves and crisis is by no means the inevitable outcome. We learn to live with our wounds, like old grumbling appendices that are never dealt with — but we pay the price. Sometimes, too, over the years a very gradual healing takes place. The pain simply subsides with love and affirmation and a very slow and entirely undramatic process of re-integration takes place. But for some, in certain situations, the pain becomes too much, and we feel a moment has arrived when there is asked of us some greater degree of honesty and offering. Our own strategies for survival grow stale and wearisome; we begin to see through them and lose the will to maintain them; the damage done to ourselves and others becomes too much to bear, and with the expectation borne of faith — or desperation — that some new and better self may be found beyond, we sense that no longer may we avoid facing up to what is really going on.

This is part of 'the second conversion', when 'everything seems to fall apart'.[50] It is the slow allowing of what has been covered up to emerge, what has been hidden to come into the light, what has lain buried to be exposed, only perhaps to find that all the time we were wrestling with something that had grown out of all proportion — indeed was even an illusion! Such can be the relief after tears, the laughter, the humour of healing! The Hindus talk of sin in these terms, using the word *maya* meaning illusion. Though in its *effects* devastatingly real and destructive, in *origin* the thing which we fear is revealed as in illusion — it doesn't really exist! We find we have been wrestling with phantoms.

This sense of wrestling with an illusion seems too to have been part of Merton's experience. In the journal he writes of 'a spring of new life, a peace and happiness that I had not known before and which subsisted in the face of nameless, interior terror,' and he continues, 'in this journal I have described the peace and not the terror . . . because as time went on, the peace grew and the terror vanished. It was the peace that was real, and the terror that was an illusion.'[51]

Disintegration

Such experience of the slow eruption of nameless fears into consciousness may well constitute the retrieving of part of our very selves, part of us which has been lost and for which we have gone hesitatingly but out of necessity, in search. Such an inner quest can be the most profound part of the personal search. Sometimes it is done alone, sometimes with the aid of friends, therapists or counsellors, always with the exploring Spirit, whose name is love and who does indeed want *everything* that we are. But such experience which is at the end of the day all about our soul's health, and a process of re-creation, can feel like precisely the opposite — like disintegration, crucifixion. It is a 'submarine earthquake'. It is very bewildering. With it quite irrational fears and anxieties can come to the surface disturbing the calm. We do not know what is going on. That is why the presence of a trusted friend can be so important. It is a time of a loss of comfort and of all subjective consolation; it is an experience of struggle with nameless enemies; it is a time of going through the motions of life, of routine, of religion. It is an experience that can yield quiet desperation and the cry 'where are you O God?' can be drowned in the midst of the clamour within.

In this desolate pilgrimage, there is no quick-fix. As we discover that the journey of joyful faith has somehow been transformed, without permission, into a hostile wilderness, the temptation is to deaden anxiety, re-inforce inner defences, and seek distraction while what is needed is the courage to stay with the experience, and struggle to believe good news even in the face of the persistence and the noisy racket of the bad. Merton's experience suggests to us three levels of the soul's response to this kind of onslaught. First, fight: 'I was summoned to battle with joy and with fear,' he writes and on New Year's Day 1950 he describes a walk in 'bare woods and driving rain . . .' and writes of the countryside itself in hostile terms: 'I saw the steep, savage hills, covered with black woods and half buried in the storm that was coming at me from the south-west. And ridges travelled away from this centre in unexpected directions. I said, "Now you are indeed alone. Be prepared to fight the devil." '52 There is a need to come to grips with the raw material of experience and personal history and to wrestle with these demons come what may. We are willing to go anywhere, to talk with friends, counsellors, therapists. Energy runs high in this determination to wrestle with our particular angel of death.

And then his experience suggests a second more passive kind of response. Such can be the inner turmoil, that we find ourselves grasping hold of any word of comfort *given* from outside, any description of our situation that fits — from a book, a film, a play, even a song, and any word of comfort that comes in the midst of that description. For religious people, the Bible, the Psalms and the Liturgy which often talk of holding on and believing in the midst of affliction are important. Merton writes of the comfort and meaning given to him from Psalm 54 chanted in the night Office:

> My heart is troubled within me: and the fear of death has fallen upon me.
> Fear and trembling are come upon me: and darkness has covered me. And I said: Who will give me wings like a dove and I will fly away and be at rest?
> Lo, I have gone far off, flying away; and I abode in the wilderness.
> I waited for him that hath saved me from pusillanimity of spirit and a storm.

He writes: 'All five lines are truer of my life than anything I have ever written, and this gives me great confidence in the liturgy. This is the secret of the Psalms. Our identity is hidden in them.'[53] Perhaps what is particularly important here is the experience of having the inner condition affirmed and recognised and met in a word that is given, or a passage read coming from outside your own experience. Many can recall moments of being spoken to at a time when they have been acutely vulnerable, defences gone, open to life or death, comfort or condemnation. I remember as a student at theological college reading Paul Tillich's sermon 'You are accepted' from his book *The Shaking of the Foundations*. In and through it I recognised myself, and was enabled to hear at a level that was more than just rational understanding what was most needed. Tillich writes of the meaning of grace:

> Grace strikes us when we are in great pain and restlessness. It strikes us when we walk through the dark valley of a meaningless and empty life. It strikes us when we

feel that our separation is deeper than usual because we
have violated another life, a life which we loved, or from
which we were estranged. It strikes us when our disgust
for our own being, our indifference, our weakness, our
hostility, and our lack of direction and composure have
become intolerable to us. It strikes us when year after
year, the longed-for perfection of life does not appear,
when the old compulsions reign within us as they have
for decades, when despair destroys all joy and courage.
Sometimes at that moment a wave of light breaks into
our darkness, and it is as if a voice were saying: 'You
are accepted. *You are accepted*, accepted by that which is
greater than you, and the name of which you do not
know. Do not ask for the name now; perhaps you will
find it later. Do not try to do anything now; perhaps
later you will do much. Do not seek for anything; do not
perform anything; do not intend anything. Simply accept
the fact that you are accepted!'[54]

And then Merton's journal suggests a third kind of
response to the experience of spiritual disintegration. The
word response is not appropriate for the overwhelming
sense is of powerlessness and the individual simply suffers.
Merton uses the image of drowning: 'My soul was cringeing
and doubling up and consciously getting ready for the next
tidal wave . . .' The only response possible here is one of
waiting, waiting in a hellish darkness. For those who suffer
in this kind of way, and it can happen to quite 'normal'
people at some stages of their life, it is truly an experience
of crucifixion. The message from Merton's journal and the
experience of others is that in and through this experience
there is, paradoxically, hope.

As we look at Merton's journal in this way, offering us
as it does the outline of a pattern of spiritual disintegration
and rebirth, it is important to see this as part of the whole.
There were entries when he writes of peace and order. The
disintegration was slow and spasmodic. No person could
stand this kind of onslaught and remain sane or even survive. There is a need for rest and intervals in the work of

purging. The experience of this kind of struggle is often intermittent and comes in waves, or is triggered only from time to time. Often it is interwoven with periods of grace, warmth, sunshine, and peacefulness.

Loneliness Transfigured

We have concentrated predominantly in this reflection on the darkness but as we have seen, light dawned too in and through it. We need to note the joyful exclamation: '. . . for the first time, I began to know what it means to be alone.' Merton interprets and explains his 'new' solitude as at long last an escape from the impure tainted and wordy ego that *was* Thomas Merton. He is on the journey into the new identity which God has stored up for him. The disintegration has been the breaking away from the old self-dramatising ego. This is his own self-understanding, and becomes a dominant theme in all his later writings. And yet the other seemingly contradictory interpretation of his experience continues to suggest itself: far from fleeing from himself he had perhaps finally confronted and dissolved the illusory and hidden childhood fears which he had previously fled from, fears which themselves had sustained the 'false self' of Thomas Merton. In the process the dread of deep loneliness was transformed into the bliss of profound solitude. All this would teach us that the task of transforming loneliness — a fundamental reality for every human being — into solitude, is the beginning of any mature spiritual journey — and paradoxically any ability to create community.

Loneliness transfigured into solitude where we meet God within us — Being itself — and then journey with him into the future, this is at the heart of the second conversion. It is accomplished both through knowing and loving ourselves and our own pasts through and through at whatever cost, and then leaving ourselves behind and learning the way of 'not knowing', abandoning the 'false self' and trusting for the gift of the 'true self' in Christ, whose name is compassion. This is the challenge and the gift that Thomas Merton shares with us. To this deeper journeying we now turn.

Chapter 6: The Roots of Protest

Using Merton's life and experience as a paradigm, and having in mind the pattern of the Exodus, we are trying to understand what may be entailed in the personal search for the Kingdom. Thus far we have touched on two levels of conversion. The first, to an ideal, a dream, powered often by a kind of certainty. In a state of innocent conviction the new believer feels that he or she has triumphantly arrived at the promised land itself. *The Seven Storey Mountain*, and many of the early entries in *The Sign of Jonas* exude this sense of triumph and arrival. Written with Merton's genius for words, it is powerfully moving and the result was that the autobiography was an instant bestseller. But the dark side of such certainty can be a hard and even arrogant disdain for the non-Christian world from which the new believer feels that they have escaped. This is the first conversion. It may cause embarrassment later but in the lives of many its importance cannot be denied, and whether we like it or not it is the first of many steps. Alan Jones likens it to the call of the first disciples who foresook all and followed Jesus without having any idea 'of the pain and the cost and the glory of their discipleship'.[1] Perhaps the main thing to note is that it is just a first step, and therefore a beginning, and necessarily superficial, with the self remaining largely unchanged — it has simply been clothed with religion. That is perhaps why new Christians are often so unattractive and frequently rather fragile. Religion has produced new loyalties, new activities, and often a lot of new noise, but as yet little disturbance or growth below the surface. So in later years we look back with both anguish and embarrassment. As we have seen, Merton himself wrote later that the young author of *The Seven Storey Mountain* was dead and in a later writing he referred to his earlier self as that 'superficially pious, rather rigid and somewhat narrow-minded young monk'.[2]

This first stage of spiritual life cannot last, at least if there is any growth. Either the exuberant new believer gives way gradually to something deeper, or if this religious self is both superficial and fragile, it may simply collapse. The house built on sand may have to fall before it can touch the rock beneath. The believer begins to experience his new and easy hope being eaten away by inner doubt. An unasked for pain and cost in this discipleship asserts itself, and he finds the doctrine of the cross and the resurrection is transmuted: from being an external article of faith to be discussed or proclaimed, it becomes an internal struggle of life and death, silently suffered. We find we are led, not into a promised land but a desert, and the desert is our own soul. There we are met by the wounds and terrors of our own past, which half consciously and half not, have mauled and battered us. We find, despite ourselves, we are entering painfully into our own unique personal inheritance, and as we learn to say yes to the totality of our own history and are enabled to experience that which was once denied and disowned, we are given the gift of ourselves. This is the second conversion. 'I cannot discover God in myself and myself in him,' wrote Merton, 'unless I have the courage to face myself exactly as I am . . .'[3] The meaning of grace, wrote Paul Tillich, is in the courage to 'accept the fact that you are accepted'. In Protestant language, justification through faith in God's grace alone.

Contemplation and Action

Beyond this though is a third conversion and a further journey, paradoxically now a movement not into ourselves but away from ourselves into a kind of emptiness where there lies the promise of a further discovery: the gift or our truest and deepest self. Merton writes: 'The salvation I speak of is not merely a subjective psychological thing — a self-realisation in the order of nature . . . it is an objective and mystical reality, the finding of ourselves in Christ, in the Spirit . . . this includes . . . and perfects the natural self-realisation which it to some extent presupposes.'[4] This is the third conversion, the continuation of the way we have already learnt, a deeper following into the desert, and it is this way above all that Merton beckons us to follow in. Having entered into our adult selves, and for some that can be a natural and almost painless process, this third stage demands a leaving of self in the sense of all self-affirmation, self-promotion and self-concern, and is a call to a radical emptiness, poverty, silence and inner solitude, and to some kind of deep waiting and listening for the promptings of the Spirit that lead to action in the life of the world. The dual emphasis in this third stage is on a deepening of the life of contemplation prompting action and service in the world. 'The spiritual principle is that action and service in the world proceed from a fullness of soul that is the result of contemplation.'[5] At the end of *The Sign of Jonas* Merton reflects: 'God sits in the ruins of my heart' (contemplation) 'preaching his Gospel to the poor' (service and action).

This third conversion, this deepening of contemplation, is the continuing of the desert journey leading us back into the world, but now seen differently, and the challenging of the gods and idols that rule there. If the desert is our own soul, the promised land we discover is not some other-worldly dream of religious bliss separated off from the world around, but in fact our own land, our own country and our own society — seen now through the sand blown eyes ·of the desert traveller who has found freedom from the illusions that the world pursues, illusions that have been met and conquered in his own soul.

In the 1950s and 60s, Merton's journey took him this full circle back into the life and struggles of the world he had turned from. There is one passage in *Conjectures of a Guilty Bystander* where he writes of this in terms of a dramatic conversion, almost a Damascus road experience, scales falling from the eyes. He writes how one day:

In Louisville, at the corner of Fourth and Walnut, in the center of the shopping district, I was suddenly over-whelmed with the realisation that I loved all those people, that they were mine and I theirs, that we could not be alien to one another even though we were total strangers. It was like waking from a dream of separate-ness, of spurious self-isolation in a special world, the world of renunciation and supposed holiness. The whole illusion of a separate holy existence is a dream. Not that I question the reality of my vocation, or of my monastic life: but the conception of 'separation from the world' that we have in the monastery too easily presents itself as a complete illusion . . . we are in the same world as everybody else, the world of the bomb, the world of race hatred, the world of technology, the world of mass media, big business, revolution, and all the rest. We take a different attitude to all these things, for we belong to God. Yet so does everybody else belong to God. . . . This sense of liberation from an illusory difference was such a relief and such a joy to me that I almost laughed out loud. And I suppose my happiness could have taken form in the words: 'Thank God, thank God that I *am* like other men, that I am only a man among others.' . . . I have the immense joy of being man, a member of a race in which God Himself became incarnate. . . . And if only everybody could realise this! But it cannot be explained. There is no way of telling people that they are all walking around shining like the sun.[6]

Merton was to live out this turning *to* the world with the same extraordinary mental energy that he had originally brought to his turning *from* the world. Throughout the 60s until his death in December 1968, he was to grapple through books, articles, correspondence and a large inter-national network of contacts with those issues that were shaping and distorting the life and social consciousness of America and indeed the whole western world. With intense probing insight he exposed the questions that lie at the heart of modern western culture. In the process he redefined the role of the monk: 'In reality the monk abandons the world only in order to listen more intently to the deepest and most neglected voices that proceed from its inner depth.'[7]

For us in this search what is important is to make the connections, the connections between spirituality and social involvement, prayer and protest, contemplation and action. We are not seeing here a simple story of monk suddenly turned social activist, man of prayer pushing that aside and becoming impatient man of action, pious contemplative walking out of the monastery to become a questioning radical. Merton's choosing of the world was the fruit and expression and outworking of his prayer and solitude. The two are one, they go hand in hand and cannot be separated. In this study our concern is the personal search, we are seeking to discern the processes of spiritual formation as seen in him, but which are in different ways true for us all. Briefly we need then to trace, through a sample of his many writings, his journey, and deepening of contemplation, leading to social involvement. It is a journey from the very personal traumas and triumphs of the early period to the free-wheeling, pungent jottings, articles, and explorations of the later Merton, the man who has identified perhaps more clearly than any other in our time the spiritual roots of social protest.

Monica Furlong writes that Merton's recognition of the importance of solitude was perhaps the most important discovery he made at Gethsemani. It was 'a kind of pivot on which the rest of his life turned'.[8] His writer's block disappeared, and there emerged in the early 50s some of his deepest writings on prayer. Two Exodus books, *Ascent to Truth* (subtitled *The Cloud and the Fire*) and *Bread in the Wilderness*, a meditation on the Psalms, mapped out the route ahead. In *Ascent to Truth* (1951) — Merton's one attempt at more systematic writing — he chose to explore the writing of St John of the Cross, the sixteenth century Spanish mystic and teacher of the dark knowledge of God. Though Merton nods in the direction of concern for the world and reminds us that St John 'far from telling us to hate the world is teaching us the only way to love and understand it',[9] the main theme here is still the personal search, in which the way ahead lies in the willingness to face what Merton sees as a strange and terrifying inner emptiness that exists at the heart of each one of us. He writes of the fear that overwhelms the silent lonely contemplative stripped of all distraction as . . . 'a huge agonising void in which the soul is turned inside out by its own nothingness and by the emptiness of all things . . . contemplation descends on us now no longer like dew but like a desert wind, smothering our whole being in fire and sand.'[10] Merton knows his subject in the only way that a writer on prayer could know it, through experience: 'The only way to true life,' he writes, 'is a kind of death. The man who feels the attraction of the Divine Truth and who realises he is being drawn out of this visible world into an unknown realm of cloud and darkness, stands like one whose head spins at the edge of a precipice.'[11] He writes of 'metaphysical anguish' in the face of nothingness, and — reminding us that the key word is 'desire' — he quotes directly the brutally simple lines of St John of the Cross:

> In order to have pleasure in everything
> Desire to have pleasure in nothing
> In order to arrive at possessing everything
> Desire to possess nothing
> In order to arrive at being everything
> Desire to be nothing
> In order to arrive at knowing everything
> Desire to know nothing . . . [12]

However, contrary to what we may fear, the result, he assures us, of this mysterious *via negativa* is not destruction and desolation but rather some kind of extraordinary visitation and indwelling. He writes 'the contemplative is repeatedly made aware of this tremendous stranger dwelling within him'.[13] In what is a personal epiphany, we are met by Another.

A New Identity

The same principle of spiritual transformation is explored in *Bread in the Wilderness* (1953), an appropriate title for a book that is about a personal exodus. In one section entitled 'Transformation in discovery', he writes of a new identity given through an experience of self-loss. It is 'a kind of death and sea-change, operated as it were at the bottom of a spiritual ocean . . . we are transformed in the midst of discovery . . . our spirit cracks the wall of its tomb with something of the power Christ shed into our souls on the morning of His Resurrection. Fear has been turned into fortitude. Anguish has become joy without somehow ceasing to be anguish, and we triumph over suffering not by escaping it but by completely accepting it . . . more than that, we ourselves have become Someone else. We remain ourselves, fully ourselves. Yet we are aware of a new principle of activity. We are fulfilled by an Identity that does not annihilate our own, which is ours and yet is "received". It is a Person eternally other than ourselves who identifies Himself perfectly with ourselves. This Identity is Christ, God.'[14]

In a third book, *Seeds of Contemplation*, (1949 and re-issued in revised form in 1961) he writes of the experience not so much as an encounter, but in more dynamic terms of discovering a new source of energy that is somehow effortless. Always though the way is through solitude, emptiness. In the meditation 'Learn to be alone' he writes, 'the truest solitude is not something outside you . . . it is an abyss opening up in the centre of your own soul . . . the one who has found solitude is empty, as if he had been emptied by death. He has advanced beyond all horizons. There are no directions left in which he can travel. This is a country whose centre is everywhere and whose circumference is nowhere. You do not find it by travelling but by standing still. Yet it is in this loneliness that the deepest activities begin. It is here that you discover act without motion, labour that is profound repose, vision in obscurity, and, beyond all desire, a fulfillment whose limits extend to

infinity.' From this potent description he goes on practically to suggest specific ways that the lay person might go
about exploring this solitude. 'There should be at least a
room, or some corner where no-one will find you and
disturb you or notice you . . .'[15]

This may seem strange to us in our more busy prosaic
and everyday life. And yet while Merton writes as a mystic
drawing on the mystical tradition, such an experience, such
a gift, is not reserved for members of religious communities
alone. This intense experience of the Kingdom, like the
Kingdom itself in the parables of Jesus, is potentially an
experience for *all*, and on reflection, all of us will have
known from time to time something of the reality of which
he writes although we may experience it in very different
ways and it is not easy to put into words.

And so, again and again, throughout the writings of the
50s and 60s, using a variety of images, Merton continues
to pursue and deepen and explore the same paradox. Sometimes, as above, the image is of a personal epiphany and
encounter or the tapping of a new source of energy; often
it is spatial — he writes of the discovery of 'an inner
ground'.[16] In one place, echoing the *Song of Songs* he draws
on an animal image: the true self (and that is what he is
writing about) is like 'a very shy wild animal that never
appears at all whenever an alien presence is at hand, and
comes out only when all is peaceful, in silence, when he is
untroubled and alone.'[17]

However expressed, the experience is fundamentally the
same, the gift of our own unique life and identity given to
us not through the affirmation and promotion of ourselves
but rather the reverse, through emptiness and darkness
and anonymity and silence — a kind of death. It is there,
in such a desert, that God meets us.

Finally, in this brief sample of a few of the key writings
which mark his journey, it is important to highlight what
is perhaps his most colourful book, *Conjectures of a Guilty
Bystander* (1965). It is a kaleidoscopic collection of jottings
and entries in which the themes of contemplation and
prayer mingle with cryptic, sardonic and frequently very

amusing observations and meditations on the monastic life, nature, other religions and the needs and issues and agonies of contemporary culture and society.

In the midst of this rich blossoming of writing, far too numerous to encapsulate here, our question is, what is the relationship between on the one hand this inner life and journey, this 'transformation in discovery' of the desert way, which was continued and deepened until the day he died, and on the other hand, his growing involvement in the life of society which we shall look at in a moment. How does the one illuminate the other? What is the nature of the connection? The tragedy is that so often contemplation and action, prayer and social responsibility, are seen not as two aspects of the one life of discipleship but as opposites, even contradictions. There are those whose calling is to a life of prayer, and there are those who feel called to engage, in Christ's name, in social protest and action. Often the former are valued while the latter may easily be disowned and dismissed. Whether or not this happens, prayer and action are usually thought of separately whereas they should be as one. In his writings and in his own person, Merton unites them, but how?

As we have seen at the heart of his personal journey was an experience of at-one-ment, the discovery of a new personal identity in God which is given. In St Paul's phrase: 'It is not I who live, but Christ who lives in me' (Gal 2:20). In sharp contrast, the key experience that lies at the root of sin is the opposite — alienation. Merton's thinking about society grew out of these two opposites, atonement and alienation, which he defined in personal terms as 'the true self' and 'the false self'. It is his idea of 'the false self' which best offers the key to his understanding of society and social protest. The false self is the self that is alienated; it is the self internally at war; the self that is in flight and separated from its own ground, the at-one-ment with the life of God. 'Every one of us,' he writes 'is shadowed by an illusory person: a false self. This is the man that I want myself to be but who cannot exist, because God does not know anything about him. And to be unknown of God is altogether too much privacy. My false and private self is the one who wants to exist outside the reach of God's will and God's love — outside of reality and outside of life. And such a self cannot help but be an illusion.'[18]

Lacking any substance in reality, this illusory self is in flight into all manner of collective illusions. 'Illusions', 'fictions', 'falsehoods', 'distractions', were favourite words Merton constantly used to describe ideologies, belief systems, and collective structures of meaning which hold sway in our public life and in which this 'false self' can lose itself in the collective tide of 'mass man'. By 'mass man', he meant the man who follows the herd and conforms to the power of fictions, or in another form of the same unreality, opts out and self-consciously seeks to affirm, to build, to fabricate, his own autonomous self by being 'different'. Both are forms of evasion from the crucial struggle to seek and find and receive the gift of personhood, our own true life in God. ' "The world" is constituted by the illusions, the myths, the prejudices, and all the mental fictions with which man torments himself and from which Christ came to deliver him.'[19] In *Contemplative Prayer* perhaps his clearest statement on prayer published after his death in 1969 he writes: '. . . society itself, institutional life, organisation, "the approved way", may in fact be encouraging us in falsity and illusion. The deep root of monastic "dread" is the inner conflict which makes us guess that in order to be true to God and to ourselves we must break with the familiar, established and secure norms and go off into the unknown.'[20] One example is a passage on freedom in *Conjectures of a Guilty Bystander* where he caricatures a popular modern myth — what he calls 'the myth of momentous choice'. He lampoons and exposes the modern executive man 'the myth of the man of decision, enlightened, determined, calculating the pros and cons, jutting out his jaw and ready to go — this is our consolation for being passive, petulant, confused, ineffectual, dominated by routines.' Merton shows how in our consumer culture we perpetuate this myth of strength and decision and choice, while it is in reality a disguise . . . 'for while we have in fact been talking our heads off about freedom we have in fact surrendered to unfreedom . . . our pitiable confusion is due to our total submission to desire: not desire in its strong and passionate form (as we would like to imagine) but desire in a weak, erratic, querulous, resentful, sub-human caricature. This desire seems strong because it can express itself in a symbolic use of powerful machines (the high-powered car), but in reality it is flabby and dependent on things, on commodities, on money, on artificial stimulation.'[21] So where do we go to find true freedom? By learning 'to admit *values which we fear*, from which we are trying to escape. Values like solitude, inner silence, reflective communion with natural realities, simple and genuine affection for other people, admission of our need for these things, admission of our need for contemplation.'[22]

The same theme of man — the false self — in flight into collective and dangerous illusions occurs repeatedly in *Raids on the Unspeakable* (1966), one of Merton's favourite books. In a meditation he writes chillingly of mankind 'being haunted by the demon of emptiness. And out of this unutterable void come the armies, the missiles, the weapons, the bombs, the concentration camps, the race riots, the racist murders, and all the other crimes of mass society.'[23]

While Merton never attempted a systematic analysis of the nature of evil, for this profoundly religious thinker, the fundamental root of the disordered and destructive world is to be found in the personal arena, in the self, alienated and in flight from God, the ground of its true life, and fabricating the illusions that it needs and feeds off. This is not to say that he believed that changing society was simply a matter of transforming individuals. Merton was not naive, his writing shows he was aware of the complex nature of society, that sin is structural as well as personal and he encouraged the building of institutional structures that would enhance and serve personal and human flourishing. But nevertheless, fundamentally he saw the root of evil as being in the individual and collective flight from, and dread of, emptiness, nothingness, non-being. 'Where is the power of error? We find it was after all not in the city, but in ourselves.'[24]

This fundamental theme of his thought, the nature of the true and false self, is explored in depth in James Finlay's book *Merton's Palace of Nowhere*. To describe the false self, Finlay uses the image of a pebble skimming across the surface of the sea: 'like stones skipped across the surface of the water we are kept skimming along the peripheral, one-dimensional fringes of life', kept moving by the fear of what lies beneath in the hidden depths of the ocean. To discover the true self requires us to become still and to sink 'into the unknown depths of God's call to union with himself'.[25] But this requires the loss of all that the false self knows and clings to and the exposing of illusions. This task of exposing and enabling humankind to *see*, to wake up, to be born out of the 'womb of collective illusion' is uniquely, Merton believed, the task of the monk and the prophet, the marginal man, the man who has dared to be alone and has 'come to see that the "emptiness" and "uselessness" which the collective mind fears and condemns are necessary conditions for the encounter with truth.'[26]

As he penetrated ever more deeply into the theme of alienation and illusion, both personal and collective, Merton was a man released and transformed. With his usual vitality he set himself to understand and grapple with the issues of contemporary life. What preoccupied him particularly were: issues of war and the dangerous 'fictional thinking' that had led to the build up of weapons of mass destruction; issues of race and the myth of racial superiority; and the unmasking of the illusory destructive alienated nature of materialist consumer society. He wrote extensively, developed an enormous correspondence and in 1964 led a retreat at Gethsemani on the spiritual roots of protest in which among others the Berrigan brothers took part — later they were imprisoned for acts of civil disobedience over the Vietnam War. Though unable himself to take direct part in active protest, Merton, from his hermitage was in touch with and an inspiration to, a movement of radical social protest in and beyond the Catholic Church.

While war and the threat of nuclear destruction, race and anti-semitism, and the Vietnam War were all pressing concerns, his over-riding protest was directed towards our whole western way of life. Again alienation was the key to his thinking. He saw society as adrift from the inner ground of meaning and believed this contrasted with the mediaeval religious hegemony which had spoken its unifying message of the life of man under God through the architecture and art of Catholic Europe. That architecture was 'sacramental' he wrote, 'now I live in a world which is to some extent bare of all such meanings and such signs.'[27] He believed that in our culture we have lost the sense of the taste of God, of the transcendent, and in our estrangement we have fabricated destructive myths that oppress and threaten us all. These must be unmasked and individuals and societies challenged to face the fear and hollowness that lies close to the surface.

The nature of the repentance, the *metanoia* he was calling for, was threefold. First, to expose illusions and this he proceeded to do with irony and humour as well as a profound sense of tragedy — note for example his poem 'Original Child Bomb'[28] about the dropping of the atomic bomb on Hiroshima, and his meditation in memory of Adolph Eichmann which exposes how near we all are to totalitarian thinking.[29] Second, to call men and women and communities to wake up, to see, to come truly alive through a deeper contemplative life. And thirdly, to encourage the building of structures, institutions, and understandings of work, democracy and for him monastic life, that enhance and do not destroy or undermine life lived at the human scale.

However, whilst encouraging action and protest, he was wary of activism. Life needs emptiness, rest, gentleness — he warned against the danger of always doing. He also warned against utopian thinking even when in supposedly good causes for this opens the way to totalitarian forces. A new social order could not be prescribed by any ideology. He believed this would be an avoidance of the painful task that men and women face in their own personal and social responsibility, an escape from openness to the emptiness and givenness of life as it unfolds, and the struggle to be human and slowly build human structures. He knew life was an untidy, painful and yet potentially glorious journey and struggle at the heart of which must remain the vocation to contemplation and prayer drawing on the wisdom of all religious traditions and leading to the exposing of collective illusions.

The Human Man

Throughout Merton's thought his priority is that the political must serve the needs of the truly personal. The things of Caesar must serve the vulnerable and tender things of God. Towards the end of his life in the hermitage his personal direction was simply to live as a man — 'the "human" man . . . who had attempted to recover "measure", to be happy in the special sense of the man who is attempting to live not just in and for the ego, but with his gaze directed beyond himself.'[30] The marks of this were simplicity, a life lived with a larger measure of solitude and contemplation, a profound relationship with nature, the pursuit of justice and a deep concern for everyman — as 'everyman is potentially Christ'. This concern means an attack on poverty 'because we have no right to let our brother live in want, or in degradation, or in any form of squalor whether physical or spiritual. In a word, if we really understood the meaning of Christianity in social life we would see it as part of the redemptive work of Christ, liberating man from misery, squalor, sub-human living conditions, economical and political slavery, ignorance, alienation.'[31]

Though never constructed in a systematic way — Merton wasn't that kind of writer — aspects of his social vision are scattered throughout his work. He was concerned with dignity in the place of work, the importance of as open a democracy as possible, with the dangers of nationalism, and with, as we have seen, the myths and destructive-

ness of technological urban society. Our concern is not to
explore this now. In the last section we shall be looking at
what discipleship may mean in our own society. Here we
need to note sufficient of the outline of his thought to
appreciate the extent of the transformation that had
occurred since the 10th December 1941 when he entered
the monastery and slammed its door on the world. In this
turning back and immersion in the struggles of that world,
he has mapped out a path we can follow for our personal
and social search, and at the heart of it is an experience of
prayer that puts question marks against so much in our
own religious lives.

Merton died — electrocuted by accident — in Bangkok
on 10th December 1968 while on a visit to the East.[32] He
had gone to explore and build bridges of understanding
between Christian mysticism and the contemplative traditions of Asia — particularly Buddhism. He believed with
men and women of all religious faiths that a humble
acknowledging of our own finitude, and radical need, and
weakness, together with a deepening of the contemplative
dimension in all life, were the only things that would save
the world from its own destruction and insanity. Twenty
years after his death, there is no reason to believe that he
was not speaking the truth.

Reflection

'The spiritual principle is that action and service in the
world proceed from a fullness of soul that is the result of
contemplation.' 'Fullness of soul' — what does it mean?
This third phase of conversion challenges us as we have
not yet been challenged with the question of prayer and
contemplation. What does it mean to pray? What does it
mean to struggle with the challenge, the demand, the fear
of contemplative prayer? Perhaps the best thing the reader
could do would be to contemplatively read Merton's own
book on this — his 'last testament'[33] — published just after
his death, in 1969. And yet though we gain much from it,

he writes as a monk primarily for monks and that's not what most of us are, or are ever likely to be.

For *Us* to Pray?

And so in this reflection, we shall try to be altogether more homely, asking in quite practical terms from the perspective of people who are not monks or hermits, but members of families, people with demanding jobs and lives and social obligations immersed in the noise and racket of contemporary society, what does it mean to try to pray, what does it mean *for us* to pray?

Of course there is a sense in which we may feel we know already, perhaps too well how to pray. We may feel we have heard an awful lot of praying and we are really very tired of it. Prayer, imposed upon us by well meaning earnest adults has been with us for as long as we can remember. Most of us have memories of bed-time prayers, school prayers, prayers in church or chapel, prayers sonorously intoned as part of national life, state and civic occasions. We have been given books on prayers, recited prayers, read prayers and even made up our own said prayers. Praying like this, praying as *wordy activity* , asking, cajoling, thanking, confessing, addressed to a distant sleepy God whom we vaguely assume is there . . . this kind of praying is all too drearily familiar to us.

This is not what is meant by contemplative prayer. This kind of praying may well have its place, in school, childhood, national life and in time of crisis or change — birth, marriage, death. It may also perform important functions, of calming, ordering, legitimating, controlling, reassuring and soothing. But it remains a pale reflection of the kind of praying that we are challenged now to engage in. 'What matters today,' writes Alan Ecclestone in his chapter on praying from his book *The Night Sky of the Lord*, 'is our willingness to begin again.'[34] Ecclestone writes of prayer as an effort, a struggle, a search to 'penetrate to the reality of human experience'. If we are to find 'fullness of soul', a new spiritual energy and vision and a capacity to stay awake and see what is really going on, this will very likely involve an altogether new kind of praying. Put in theological terms the question is: how are we to enter and discover and dwell in the life of God — *as our life?* 'It is not I who live,' says St Paul, 'but Christ who lives in me.' Only prayer that aims at this, the inter-penetration of human and divine, the fusion of man or woman and God, only prayer that wrestles with this can be prayer that is adequate to the task of seeing, and the uncovering and exposing of the roots of our personal and social lives.

Although we have already looked at the process of conversion in its early stages, how is it that we have not so far faced this question of prayer? Perhaps it is that at the time of the first conversion prayer somehow does not become this kind of struggle to break through to something that is altogether new, just doesn't have this feel about it. Certainly prayer was important, both as a child and in the first flush of conversion. We needed to learn how to pray. But we were told there was a right way, and we were taught how to do it. The dominant note in this first stage is clarity, certainty, the faith well-defined, each section of belief and practice clearly marked out, an objective body of truth separate from us — something that we had to learn. As well as sermons, Bible studies and lectures, 'how to pray' books and Bible reading notes were part of this learning. In the evangelical tradition there is the 'quiet time', a short period set aside every day for prayer. I remember it as a time for reaffirming with the help of Bible reading notes, the clear structure of belief I had grasped, and then launching out in an effort to praise the God who was utterly other to the sinful me but who had forgiven me in Christ; to examine behaviour and confess wrong doing; to give thanks; and to ask. Intercession was important, for change and conversion and healing, for friend and enemy and world — for God's will to be done. Though called the 'quiet time', the trouble was it was not very quiet, and involved a lot of noisy activity — a daily spiritual hurdling course — each stage needing to be properly gone through. There were of course many permutations, and prayer developed and lapsed in different ways, but perhaps the dominant and constant theme was God as Object, other than the individual, touching and healing us perhaps through Christ, but still God as *separate*.

Perhaps this is the heart of the first conversion: God as Other. He draws me, attracts me, judges me, forgives me, begins the process of cracking open my proud and hardened ego, but always he is somehow other. The first disciples followed the Jesus who was other to them, and the crowds brought the sick to him and he healed them. That is what we did in prayer and evangelism — brought our friends to Jesus. Prayer in the first conversion is the addressing of the One who is always other to us and distinct from us, to whom we bring ourselves and our world for healing. This is the distinctive emphasis — totally in tune with the Gospel story. I am reminded of a scene in Pasolini's *The Gospel According to St Matthew*. The film was made in black and white. No sentimental Jesus here but a harsh demanding figure challenging the poor slow-witted disciples with the radical demand of the Gospel. The scene was of the disciples following Jesus on a stoney track. They stumble along, a good half dozen paces behind the lean sinewy figure of Jesus striding out ahead. Every so often he suddenly turns and barks back to them the words of the Gospel, but he is always striding ahead of them and they stumbling along behind, and the gap is always there between the two. That is how I remember it felt — a struggle to keep up with this demanding restless God. In our prayers we were always saying sorry, always asking, and he was always distant. Perhaps this was always the experience of the first disciples, and seems to be confirmed by Jesus's words said to those bewildered men at the end of John's Gospel: 'It is good that I go away from you, otherwise the Holy Spirit, the advocate, the comforter, the one who dwells *within*, will not come' (John 16:7). Unless as separate from you, I go and disappear and die, the penetration will not occur, Pentecost and the third conversion will not be reached. But between this first following — sometimes glorious, sometimes bewildering — and that third stage of strange indwelling, everything will fall apart. You will all betray me, and yourselves, and they did not understand, and neither do we as it happens to us.

In the second phase, prayer as mental or verbal activity is shot to bits, it just won't work and feels increasingly hollow. Instead, our life itself becomes a prayer — a wordless plea and struggle for survival. While the crisis can take many forms it is also a time of the first fruits of the new and deeper life to appear, a time of 'groaning inwardly as we wait . . .' (Rom 8:23). In this phase we cannot pray because prayer presupposes some spiritual foundation or identity and it is precisely these foundations themselves which in this crisis are being swept away. That is what this second stage is about. All you can do is, as St Paul puts it, to wait, to hang on in the flood watching the spate of inner change remove the old familiar landmarks of experience. It feels like drowning but in reality it is that God like the thief in the night — and the night can be very black — is breaking into us, demolishing the outer self in the process. It is not easy and courage is demanded. Some lines from Christopher Fry's play *The Sleep of Prisoners* sum it up:

> The human heart can go to the lengths of God.
> Dark and cold we may be, but this
> Is no winter now. The frozen misery
> Of centuries breaks, cracks, begins to move:
> The thunder is the thunder of the floes,
> The thaw, the flood, the upstart Spring.
>
> Thank God our time is now when wrong
> Comes up to face us everywhere.
> Never to leave us till we take
> The longest stride of soul men ever took.
> Affairs are now soul size.
> The enterprise
> Is exploration into God.[35]

Though all our experience belies it — 'wrong comes up to face us everywhere' — in fact we are moving into a new experience, exploration into God within and without. But the practices and habits of prayer are taken too in the flood. At Gethsemane, the disciples could not pray but sought relief through sleep, the refuge of all whose lives have been torn apart by mental illness, depression, breakdown, unemployment. What they cannot do is pray. Christ prays for them until the flood abates and we touch some deeper rock within. 'You are Simon, you shall be Peter, the rock' (John 1:42) — but only the other side of bitter weeping. Such is the second conversion leading to the discovery of new and deeper foundations restoring prayer once again to its place as part of a way of life, but now the way *to* life itself.

As we noted at the beginning none of this happens easily. We find we repeat again and again in different form these phases in the life of the Spirit. The second conversion, the falling apart and discovery of deeper roots, has often to be gone through in different disguises as we find we have reconstructed new certainties that deny the way of faith, the way of not knowing. Nevertheless, slowly, spasmodically even if painfully, we move into the beginning of the third conversion — a deepening of faith that depends less on feeling or mood and knows more the secret of waiting, even in darkness.

Now we have to learn to pray. But how? We are no longer satisfied with the old model. We have discovered that God is not some object out there separate from us, a Supreme Being governing all things, but rather Being itself, whom we find in our own truest and deepest life . . . 'It is not I who live,' we begin faintly to know with St Paul, 'but Christ who lives in me.' But how to sustain this inner life? Slowly we begin to sense that prayer rather than being an intermittent occasional extra on the margins of our Christianity is moving inexorably to the centre. Slowly it is becoming a life and death matter for us whether or not we pray.

But how? This book did not set out to be a book on prayer. We are in search of the Kingdom yet we find that search has led us to this which is perhaps the most difficult question of all: how do we pray? We have come to realise that prayer is not just the way to the Kingdom but *is* the Kingdom. We have come to realise that prayer contains within it the very life of that Kingdom. Here is the secret of true identity hidden in God; here is the ability to see more clearly; here is the capacity to love again; here is potentially the energy to care and stay involved with people, issues, situations that feel log-jammed and hopeless. But how, how as the old models and ways have collapsed, to sustain it? We feel beyond speech, beyond words, and there is not much help.

Inner Transformation

At this point all we can do is share some of our own stumblings and false starts remembering some words of Thomas Merton: 'nothing that anyone says will be that important. The great thing is prayer. Prayer itself. If you want a life of prayer, the way to get to it is by praying.'[36] In other words in this process of what he calls later in a discussion on monasticism, 'total inner transformation',[37] each of us is on our own — 'from now on everybody stands on his own feet.'[38] Nobody can teach us to pray, all that we can do is listen to the experience of others and then go into our place alone and face the dilemmas and ways forward as best we can — trusting. That is perhaps the beginning of prayer.

And yet is it so difficult? In the same address on prayer, Merton also has words of comfort, describing praying in terms of the discovery of that which already exists: 'In prayer we discover what we already have. You start where you are and you deepen what you already have, and you realise that you are already there. We already have everything, but we don't know it and we don't experience it. Everything has been given to us in Christ. All we need is to experience what we already possess. The trouble is we aren't taking time to do so.'[39] He talks less of struggle, and more of growth, like a plant unfolding, and simply needing time. Easy and simple, yet difficult — requiring a lifetime and more.

Merton's words suggest that in this discussion there is a need to broaden the word prayer so it speaks of not just specific religious activity done at particular times but a whole way of life which is infused by the life-giving Spirit. What we are talking about in asking how do we pray, is how do we build and develop our own very particular structure and discipline for nurturing a life attentive to God in every waking moment? Prayer is not just a small piece of time set aside alone, or something said in church; prayer is searching out the life of God in every single activity we do, word we speak, decision we make, friendship we create, interest we pursue. It is a wholesale re-designing, re-fashioning and re-building of the structure that is my life and may necessitate some essential demolition work on the old.

How this occurs in each one of us will differ enormously depending on our age, personality, social background, natural interests, understanding of faith and a host of other variables. We cannot prescribe a prayer life, it has to be uniquely and individually hacked out and shaped from the raw material of our own experience and the interaction between our personal history and the understanding of the faith that we have been given. Each of us must do it for ourselves. And we should be wary of blindly following prescriptions offered by others that 'worked' for them.

Those few things necessary.

Nevertheless while we embark and make progress alone, it is possible tentatively and briefly to suggest some fundamentals — basic guidelines — that others have followed which may point the way ahead: those few things that experience suggests are necessary, to enter into the one thing that is necessary.

First *time matters*. Most people who embark on this prayer thing talk of a regular period of time — normally early in the morning — that needs to be marked out and set aside on a regular basis. It requires commitment and discipline. The ideal and norm should be every day, though there may be periods when we simply cannot sustain this because our life has become unbalanced with too much work, or illness, or some other cause that means every bit of energy is required for survival.

Second, *place*. One of the most helpful and homely books on prayer in the midst of ordinary life is *Motherhood and God*, a book written by a mother of small children about finding motherhood in God and God in motherhood. Margaret Hebblethwaite describes how in her house she made 'a prayer hole' in an under-the-stairs cupboard, a special place set aside for prayer and decorated with a few simple objects, a candle, a crucifix, some postcards. She writes: 'I need my prayer hole because I am bad at praying. I need it because I can just go in and just do nothing and then I am praying. It takes the effort out of it, and the dread, and the fear of boredom, and the distractions. It cuts down the interruptions too: when I am in my prayer hole people do not burst in on me. If they need me they call respectfully. They do not break in on that fragile vulnerable core of being that we need to let unfold gently in the sight of God'.[40]

Of course we can pray anywhere, on the top of a bus, in the supermarket, at work, at home, doing the washing up. But that doesn't alter the fact that we need special times and special places that become reference points, anchor points that we can think of and remember during the day, that offer us a framework. Some people find a nearby church, which has quiet corners, a place of refuge where they can begin this process of unfolding before God.

Third, *help from others*. While we learn to pray alone - and of course we also need prayer with others — praying must not become an isolated thing done without reference to others in the Christian community. Help can take many forms, through discussions and sharing experience with friends, through finding a spiritual director, through books. Prayer as a living evolving thread growing at the heart of our life will need all of these at different times.

Fourth, *focus*. What do we *do* in this time? While the mystics write of the praying person becoming still and silent and wordless, the spirit moving beneath the level of rational mental activity, nevertheless it is helpful to have a framework and structure for praying even if it is quite often abandoned. One form is the use of the shorter form of Morning Prayer according to the Anglican *Alternative Service Book*. It offers a simple structure of psalms and readings for everyday use — though beware. Contemplative prayer is not about reciting a lot of words, it is a search for God who is beyond all words, and we may find that one line, one phrase, one word of the psalms, repeated slowly again and again, is enough to act as the focus of that deeper effort of penetration.

In the privacy of our own place we need to let prayer unfold and realise that we are involved in something which is work and not work, effort and rest, activity and waiting, staying with the structure and willing, as people, issues and concerns present themselves, to wander off, but then to return — for prayer is primarily a struggle to enter into the life of God. In all this small practical things can make a difference — like posture. Some people use a prayer stool and so can sit back for hours. Others sit cross-legged, eastern style. Both are essentially contemplative, empty, open. A visual focus can help. The small flame of the candle symbolising the life of Christ lit before you evokes stillness and presence. And stillness matters, outward stillness with deeper breathing, leading to an inward silencing of the incessant chattering brain. Here the words are important — particularly the psalms focusing the brain on the task, the work, of digging into prayer. As we try to bring the whole self into stillness, the words — maybe one word or phrase — need to be gone over slowly, meditatively, repetition is important, the phrase being used again and again stilling the chattering anxious brain like lassooing a crazy frightened colt. The mystics speak of 'taking the head into the heart' letting the word go deeper into and below the conscious mind. Imagination is important here too. We need to use and play with the pictures and images evoked by certain biblical phrases so that they penetrate into the seams and fabric of consciousness.

We may be surprised what prayer leads to if we give it the time. Perhaps first great comfort and a profound sense of peace and stability as we learn to rest. Sometimes boredom and frustration and even a sense of shock as we realise, after prayer, that we are much worse tempered than we were before. Sometimes fear, which perhaps we should expect as we sense the emptiness and the fragility of our life, and face up to death, or are disturbed by the emergence of things and people submerged in the conscious mind which are salvaged in prayer. Sometimes clearer vision, the capacity to see. Prayer is a time to go over again the encounters with the people we have met and shall meet that day and seek to see them again, and realise the social and personal forces that they are under. In prayer we embrace them, love them, hope for them, believe in them — just as God does.

As we explore prayer like this we discover its task is to penetrate everything, and grow in different forms: individual prayer, communal prayer and retreats, and prayer with others. Each of us must find our own balance, way, pace and rhythm in this art of praying, and then check it against the knowledge and experience of others. Ultimately it is tested by its fruits, by its results, but before making judgements of ourselves or anyone else we need to remember that we begin in different places with different histories and sometimes quite severe emotional wounds that have to be worked through.

Finally, prayer needs to be nourished by other activities which are contemplative in style — themselves part of praying: music, painting, bird watching, walking, gardening, potting, poetry, and even jogging — and certainly it is possible to jog contemplatively. These can themselves be part of our prayer, part of our listening and seeking of the divine life, part of our struggle to wake up, to see, to hope and to protest against conditions and times that are cruel and barbarous.

How we grow, for prayer is growth, will differ, but staying committed to some structure for prayer is being committed to growth, to the belief that God the Creator is still at work fashioning us into our true identity and likeness, the likeness of Jesus Christ. As we move out in search of God's Kingdom beyond ourselves — and prayer must ultimately be a release from the all-consuming self — into the life of society, we must be aware of the danger of losing touch and failing to nourish this vital inner resource, for without it, work and activity become activism — sound and fury signifying very little.

PART THREE

IN SEARCH OF THE KINGDOM

And did the Countenance Divine,
Shine forth upon our clouded hills?
And was Jerusalem builded there
Among those dark Satanic Mills?
                    William Blake.

Chapter 7: A Question of Politics?

In this search for the Kingdom, let us briefly trace the path we have come. In the first part, we have seen that the promised Reign of God that the Hebrews looked for was a hope for and in *this* world, involving the very earth itself. However, the promise was not made in a moral vacuum but dependent for its fulfilment on their obedient living out, in the covenant relationship, of the *ethical* character of Yahweh, their God.

The New Testament reveals a Kingdom given a new and ultimate definition through Jesus of Nazareth. It is the gift of life itself given for all and lived out to the uttermost through and beyond death. Out of that Beyond, a new community is born in and through the Spirit where the gift of life is given and received again and again through the remembering, the re-living, and the thanksgiving of the Eucharist.

And yet while the nature of this open secret — the way through death to the gift of the Kingdom — has been revealed, the way has to be searched for again and again both personally and corporately in every society and age. Personally *and* corporately, *both* dimensions matter.

Through the journey of Thomas Merton we have explored some of the difficult terrain of the personal quest — what Jesus called 'the narrow road that leads to life' — and found the central theme to be 'identity'. The Reign of God is experienced in the gift of 'the true self' discovered by way of the death of 'the false self', But this 'true self' while requiring a measure of inner solitude to come to birth and remain nourished, is never a self in splendid isolation; we are not meant to live like twentieth century versions of the bizarre St Simeon Stylites who thought the world so corrupt that he made his home on

top of a pillar! To separate oneself in spiritual isolation is
to erect another 'false self', far more dangerous than before
simply because it thinks itself so righteous. As Merton
constantly pointed out, this inner discovery is not some
kind of a private thing that has been 'achieved', but the
discovery of the living reflection of the life of God in every
person. So it dawns that the deepest truth of our humanity
is in fact not our separation and differences as we are
constantly told, but our unity — our at-one-ment in God.
Appropriately this discovery really came home to him not
in the cloister or the church, but in a shopping centre: 'In
Louisville at the corner of Fourth and Walnut, in the centre
of a shopping district, I was suddenly overwhelmed with
the realisation that I loved all these people, that they were
mine and I theirs, that we could not be alien to one another
even though we were total strangers.' Out of this at-one-
ness is born a new way, of compassion — literally 'feeling
with'. Alive to the reflection of God within, we suffer or
flourish as one. At the end of the piece about the Louisville
shopping centre is the remarkable phrase: 'There is no way
of telling people that they are all walking round shining
like the sun.' This is the ecstatic and agonising way of
openness and contemplation that is the gift of Thomas
Merton.

Thomas Merton is one prominent voice of the twentieth
century who leads us from the personal to the corporate,
and puts the question: how in the structures of society can
we build the life of the Kingdom? As he knew well, in a
post-Marxist world, structures are unavoidable.

However to acknowledge that sin, understood as the
dislocation of a fundamental unity, is structural as well as
personal is not easy for many Christians to either accept
or cope with. It begins to sound alarmingly political. What
does it mean?

In terms of the image of the Exodus journey, the place
now arrived at is the edge of the desert. Like the Hebrews
facing the land that had been promised to them, this land
too is chaotic and dominated by alien powers. It is clear
that the focus of the search for the Kingdom now must

shift from the world within to the world without, otherwise it becomes a kind of perpetual self-indulgence. The land of promise is for all; Jerusalem has to be built in society as well as in the individual soul — that is the focus of this third part — but how?

As with the personal search there is no quick fix, no easy way of social transformation such as is sometimes suggested by mass evangelistic campaigns. The longing for rapid social transformation through the power of religion has been evident in recent years through initiatives like 'The Nationwide Festival of Light' (1972), and the 'Archbishop's Call to the Nation' (1975). These movements which take up the time and energy of large numbers of people somehow always prove disappointing because they fail to engage deeply enough with the structural — and so political nature of sin and dislocation in society.

It may be best to begin by trying to identify what is in fact going on. Broadly, three kinds of interlinked responses suggest themselves.

Three Ways of Response

First, the development of ministries of support and help towards individuals who feel personally lost. This is a continuation of the desert way, but now helping others to do their own journeying and discover their own hidden inner ground. As society as a whole continues to drift away from any common religious undergirdings, the development of personal ministries of counselling, therapy and spiritual journeying with people becomes increasingly important. The connections that Merton highlights between 'the false self' and 'a false society' would suggest that the struggle for truth within, has profound social consequences.

A second way of response is in the area of 'ambulance work', the individual support of victims. The pilgrim setting off to pick her way through the rubble of a social order increasingly in ruins is sharply alert to the cries of the trapped victims beneath the debris. It's an approach that has established a variety of organisations, for example the

Samaritans, and spawned a range of initiatives in which Christian people are engaged with others: action centres with the unemployed; welfare rights advice; housing initiatives; support for one parent families; the tradition of social and community work. Learning from the approach of community development, the emphasis is increasingly on *working with*, rather than *caring for* people.

A third response leading out of the first two is the engagement with particular issues, and the development of campaigns for change. The single issue approach which often simply assumes a basic consensus of Christian values is the dominant approach pursued by and in the structures that the churches have set up to focus social responsibility. As well as the General Synod Board for Social Responsibility, the Anglican Church now has Boards or Councils for Social Responsibility in almost every Diocese of the Church of England and similar structures exist in other denominations. These bodies produce a range of reports from working parties and special groups set up to examine particular issues. A glance at the Anglican BSR Publication list[1] gives a feel of their work, mentioning reports recently produced across a wide range, for example: Racism, Housing and Homelessness, Aids, Community Work, Responsibility for the Environment, Policing, Sunday Trading, Human Fertilisation and Embryology, Euthanasia, Transnational Corporations, Technology, Work and the Future, World Development Education, The Welfare State. Only three in the list take a broader look: *The Church of England and Politics* (1981); *Perspectives on Economics* (1984); and *Changing Britain, Social Diversity and Moral Unity*, a report on Values (1987). However, the report on the Welfare State, *Not just for the Poor* (1986), is very wide ranging.[2] Perhaps most notable among these reports in recent years were, *The Church and the Bomb*[3] (1983), which advocated unilateral moves towards nuclear disarmament, and the Report of the Archbishop's Commission on Urban Priority Areas, *Faith in the City* (1985).[4] Encouraged by the thinking being expressed in these kind of reports, and appalled and alarmed by the growing divisions within society, and the kind of weapon systems being deployed to protect this divided society, Christians individually and in groups have become deeply involved in specific issue campaigning. Church Action on Poverty and Christian CND are perhaps the two most obvious examples of this kind of involvement.

And yet despite this activity which articulates fears, protests against the status quo, and looks for a better way in specific areas of policy, the question increasingly presents itself: is this approach — in itself — sufficiently radical? Does it have sufficient roots in the Christian tradition? And does it particularly have sufficient roots to answer the criticism from the political and ecclesiastical Right that the Church is simply jumping on the faddish bandwagon of a rather shallow kind of western liberal thought at the cost of abandoning the true meaning of the gospel? This was the nub of the critique of Edward Norman in his Reith Lectures of 1978, which clearly resonated with a large number of people within and outside the Churches. In his chapter in the collection of essays published to celebrate the twenty-fifth anniversary of Honest to God, Trevor Beeson makes the same point. Looking back to the end of the 1960s he comments: 'It had become increasingly evident that the effort of that decade to move the Church towards a much greater concern for social issues had not been accompanied by an equally necessary effort to rediscover the biblical and theological foundations of such a concern . . . In consequence the criticism that the Church's pronouncements were simply of a secular character, and had no more authority than the views expressed by the leader-writer of a liberal newspaper, was not without some validity.' Looking on from the early 1970s, Beeson continues: 'The continuing failure of Church leaders to spell out the religious basis of their criticisms of particular government policies, allied sometimes to a failure to appreciate the complexity of certain social and economic problems, still makes them vulnerable to the rejoinder of the politician that they have strayed from their proper domain and that their comments are altogether unhelpful.'[5]

Put positively, the challenge is: *What are the distinctively*

Christian roots of social protest, and how do these roots, once identified, either question or directly challenge current political policies and the ideologies, the belief constructs, that lie behind policies?

We have already noted in Part Two one way of addressing this question. Merton's connection between personal and social alienation is one way of radicalism. Through his own experience, he dug down and exposed the personal roots of a false and alienated society, but in itself this is not enough. Personal alienation, the proud assertion of the autonomous ego, may give rise to an alienated society — a host of individual selves cumulatively engaged in a kind of mass Gadarene stampede — but this collective alienation then gets blessed and hardened into ideological structures and belief systems — what Merton called 'fabrications' — which themselves need to be clearly delineated and analysed and subjected to criticism from values from the tradition of thought about God.

From Issues to Ideology

So there is a need to focus on the more fundamental questions of ideology, even while recognising the importance of campaigning on specific issues. This may be seen as a fourth way of response, the difficult toughminded task of moral and theological questioning of political ideology, requiring considerable nerve as it takes the Christian right into the arena of politics and specific political programmes.

This will be the focus in this third part of this search for the meaning of the Kingdom. What follows will serve, I hope, as a brief introduction to this task; it is a process of debate and discussion that needs to involve far more people in the churches than hitherto. We shall find it is hard work, often uncongenial, and it will take us into unfamiliar territory, i.e., the debate about those political ideas and philosophies that are the major shaping forces in our common life. However, by now it should be clear that the way to the Kingdom is always through the unfamiliar; this will be true in the public realm as much as it is in all our private searchings.

Up to the end of the 1970s the need to engage in this task was perhaps less important which may account for the small amount of work that has been done in this area certainly in the British churches. Since 1945 we have enjoyed a broad social consensus that emerged out of the pre-war depression, was forged during the war itself, and found expression in the legislation that gave birth to the Welfare State in the years immediately afterwards. The Church, particularly through the work of William Temple played a significant part in defining and mapping out this consensus of values — an agreement that broadly held under different governments in Britain, both Labour and Conservative, from 1945 onwards. It was a consensus that stressed the role of the state as intervenor in society to support a mix of values of which equality and social justice were central. Precisely what level of equality was practicable and desirable, and what means should be pursued to ensure a degree of social justice were disputed, but nevertheless a rough agreement between political parties and the Church was maintained about the desirability of these values and the importance of the state's role in sustaining them. Of course, the criticism from the Left has always been that these values were never really aggressively pursued by Labour Governments and so Britain has remained a fundamentally unjust, unequal and class-ridden society.

Nevertheless while this broad political consensus held, supported as it was by a rising tide of post-war prosperity that disguised the continuing underlying inequalities, and while the values that undergirded it were paid lip service to by all as important, any Church campaigning on issues of injustice had potentially powerful moral bite — the Church was in a position to play its role as 'conscience of the nation'. Since the end of the 1970s however, for a number of complex reasons, that situation has dramatically changed, and it is only late in the day that the Church appears to be waking up to the extent of that change and so the ineffectiveness of simply assuming shared values and calling the government and the nation to return to them.

The Report *Faith in the City* which powerfully outlines the extent of poverty and social division in England, has been called theologically 'shallow', but its deficiency was more in its failure to attend sufficiently to the changing ideological context and the need effectively to address that, from the tradition of Christian social thought. The result was a report which, while highly effective in certain respects, yet had a dated feel to it from the moment it came out. It simply was not addressing the ideological world of the 1980s, and was not sufficiently helping Christians to see what kind of social order might best express Christian values, and what are the 'legitimate options'[6] now for Christians to support.

Since the publication of *Faith in the City*, the challenge to clarify the outline of a social vision related to Christian values has become pressing as those who embrace the ideology of Laissez-faire Capitalism continue in power — with very serious social consequences. In this situation, Christian social responsibility demands that hard thinking about political ideology be done. After ten years of a government of the radical Right, we can no longer assume that there is a broad consensus about the importance to be attached to certain key values in the making of public policy. In short, we have to face now, much more than we have before, the question of ideology.

But first it may be helpful to clarify some terms, and particularly this word 'ideology' — what does it mean? In his book *Christians and the Great Economic Debate*, Philip Wogaman offers a simple definition: an ideology is 'a complex weaving together of values and beliefs. It is our (often unconscious) picture of what society ought to be like'.[7] Whether we know it or not, he says, all of us do in fact think ideologically, and he locates five main ideological tendencies in the economic debates of our time: Marxian Communism, Laissez-faire Capitalism, Social Market Capitalism (the mixed economy), Democratic Socialism, and Economic Conservationism.

It has to be recognised that ideology has come to be something of a dirty word amongst intellectuals in the middle ground of politics (where the Church usually is) who like to think in a rather high-minded way that they are somehow above it all. 'He's just an ideologue', we say shaking our heads — it's an effective way of dismissing the arguments of someone we dislike. What we normally mean when we trade insults like this is that someone is ideologically rigid or blinkered, i.e., so committed to their particular understanding of values and policies that they are quite blind to the havoc and damage that they are causing — that is the peculiar blindness of ideological rigidity and 'blinkered' is a good word. But frequent examples of it in public life, should not allow the rest of us to delude ourselves that we can therefore somehow escape this contagion! We are ideological too, to the extent that we are committed to a certain mix of values in politics. Ones that might particularly matter to us might be equality, social justice, freedom, conservation. But others, for example, efficiency, competition, order, may also be necessary in a complex modern society, though they are likely to be decidedly less popular to many Christians. How we understand and mix these values will determine our ideological tendency. Of course there is nothing new in this. Ideology is no nasty modern invention of the twentieth century. The ideology that held sway in Britain for centuries was 'traditional feudalism'. Recently in a small Oxfordshire church, I came across a wall plaque commemorating one William Wickham Esq. It beautifully encapsulates the feel of a very different social ideology:

In Memory
Of WILLIAM WICKHAM Esq
Of this Parish
Who died May 28 1727
Aged 47

The Fear of God and the Love of his Country
Were the ruling Principles of his Life and Actions
As a Protestant Englishman
He was steady without Violence,
As a Husband and Father,

Indulgent without Weakness,
As a Neighbour and Friend,
Generous without Design.
The Influence of his Memory still prevails
And hence every Private Gentleman may learn
That his own depends upon the Publick Good,
And they are both servd best in the Duties of his Station.

Here values of order, hierarchy, and a particular understanding of 'The Publick Good' predominate. It's worth
noting too that its the '*Publick Good*' which defines and
determines *private* well being.

Any search for the Kingdom in society must then engage
with ideology. The question that it poses is this: how does
Christian belief about God and his purposes inform our
values, and so provide guidance towards the kind of ideology that we can say yes to, and support, and the kind of
ideology that we must say no to, and oppose? To this we
shall turn in a moment.

However first, this search needs to be set in the very
particular context of our society at the end of the 1980s
and beginning of the 1990s. In his illuminating survey of
trends in modern political theology, Duncan Forrester
makes the point that 'Political theology is contextual theology. It addresses itself to *a particular situation at a specific
time*'[8] (my italics). Arguably all theology that is true to the
way of Jesus Christ should have this 'incarnational' focus,
but it is all the more important and urgent that in a time
of severe social dislocation, the Church should curb its
tendency to pronounce in generalities and timeless truths,
and direct its understanding of God into the particular
situation before it, searching and listening for the word and
way of God here and today: 'The church must be able to
say the Word of God, the word of authority here and now,'
wrote Bonhoeffer, 'in the most concrete way possible from
knowledge of the situation. The church may not therefore
preach timeless principles, however true, but only
commandments which are true today. God is always God
to us today.'[9]

And so the first question as we attempt to come to grips with the question of ideology is: what is our 'today'? What is our political/ideological 'today' here in Britain. Before suggesting any theological responses we need briefly to remind ourselves of some of the principle characteristics of the ideological tendency that has been dominant in Britain (and the US) throughout the 1980s, and ask, what understandings of key social values are operating here?

The New Right

The political stance growing out of the political and economic philosophy generally known as 'Laissez-faire Capitalism', or 'Conservative Capitalism', or 'Neo-liberalism' — often simply known as 'The New Right' — is, in broad outline very familiar to the British public after more than ten years of a government which has been profoundly influenced by these ideas. Cutting taxes to encourage enterprise and initiative, relying on market forces in the distribution of goods and services, a much reduced role for the state . . . these ideas have been common political currency of the Thatcher years. As with any broad political ideology it would be a mistake to think of this as some kind of pure coherent theory! Behind the rather simple rhetoric is a complex political and economic philosophy with different strands and emphases. It seems clear too that some of the basic principles have often been ignored in the interests of particular groups, thus underlining the questions raised by Ronald Preston in his critique of the New Right: 'How far is this professed belief which can so often be ignored a deception? If it is, is it a conscious deception or not? In whose interests is it being advanced?'[10] This only brings home that ideologies are rarely pursued in some kind of absolute way, and are certainly not devoid of self or class interest.

Nevertheless we need to note some of the main features: three seem of particular importance. First, a re-defining and scaling down of the role of the state so that its principal functions could be defined as (a) externally, the maintenance of defence to deter aggression, and (b) internally, the preservation of the rule of Law to prevent individuals transgressing basic rights — to life, privacy, property and security. So the state is the guardian of freedom defined negatively as 'the absence of coercion'.[11] Second, a strong belief in the impersonal mechanism of the free market as the best and most efficient means of creating wealth and distributing goods and services. Third, a strong emphasis on the individual as consumer to choose and to compete.

The minimal state, the impersonal mechanism of the market, and human beings defined as 'separate and individual monads'[12] free to accumulate wealth and property. Three basic planks of New Right thinking that has led to the birth in Britain of the much vaunted 'Enterprise Culture'. Fundamental to all this there seems to be a kind of crude darwinian belief in the survival of the fittest in the economic and social jungle that is now society. 'The sole appeal,' writes Preston 'is to self-interest'[13] and the assumption would appear to be that out of the pursuit of millions of *private* self-interests somehow some conception of the *public* good is served. However the now famous utterance of the British Prime Minister that 'there is no such thing as society, only individuals and their families' must underline the doubts that already exist that politicians of the Right embrace any coherent view at all of this ancient idea.

Before looking more closely at the values of this tendency, one important belief at the root of the system needs highlighting, and that is that economics is a pure, neutral, and value-free 'science' — quite separate from moral values at all! In this view economics conforms to immutable laws and quite simply these are either obeyed or chaos results. Peter Selby refers to this as one more version of 'The Myth of Origin': '. . . we are being told, in the version of the myth of origin most common at the present time, that the operation of the economic order is also "natural", and that the increasing number of people who have lost their economic rights through unemployment are doing so because of the painful but inexorable functioning of the laws of economics. However sad it is, and those who tell us these things are weeping all the way to the bank, these natural forces have to be allowed to run their course.'[14] John Atherton in his *Faith of the Nation* quotes Von Mises, a major theoretician of The New Right: it is a 'Liberalism . . . derived from the pure sciences of economics and sociology which make no value judgements in their own spheres and says nothing about what ought to be and what is good and what is bad, but on the contrary, only ascertains what is and how it comes to be.'[15] Interestingly, Laissez-faire Capitalism and Marxism have here much in common; both claim to be 'scientific' and above values — it is this that makes them into hard ideologies, and the Christian should be alert to the strong whiff of idolatry. Economics is a complex body of knowledge but fundamentally it is to do with how we share goods and services and resources and that involves *moral* decisions. It is therefore possible to make value judgements in the sphere of economics as much as in any other of the social sciences. Atherton makes the point well: 'There can never be any other God but God.'[16]

Freedom, Social Justice, Community

If 'Ideology is a complex weaving together of values and beliefs . . .' what are the values and beliefs that undergird this tendency? In a recent paper produced by the Diocese of Winchester, Professor Raymond Plant examines the interpretation that the New Right gives to three key social values: freedom, social justice, and community. We shall look at each in turn and ask how these concepts, which are basic to any political theology, are being understood and interpreted on the Right, in ways that differ significantly from how they have been commonly understood in the Christian tradition.

First, *freedom*. Plant demonstrates how in the political vocabulary of the New Right, *freedom* to do anything is understood quite separately from the *ability* or having the *resources* to do anything; freedom and ability must be clearly distinguished and so freedom is defined negatively as 'the absence of intentional coercion'.

> ... the first conclusion to be drawn in respect of the role of government is that government can secure equal negative liberty, in the sense of securing the absence of intentional coercion to the highest degree possible by providing, applying to all citizens equally, a framework of law, which defines these boundaries, the crossing of which would lead to coercion. However, because people are not coerced by their lack of resources, *there is no duty on government to seek for a redistribution of resources in favour of the worst off in order to secure a more equal distribution of liberty.*[17] (my italics)

To drive this point home, Plant reminds us of Sir Keith Joseph's striking phrase, 'poverty is not unfreedom'.[18] This means that if you are poor — perhaps you live on a very low income, have no means of transport to visit friends or move out of your environment, cannot get a job, are deeply anxious about providing for even the basic necessities of daily living — as long as you are not intentionally coerced by anyone, including the state (and the state is almost always seen in coercive terms), then you are not 'unfree'.

Second, how does the ideology of the New Right understand the notion of *social justice* or *equality*, again key concepts in any understanding of the Kingdom of God? The question needs to be approached at the theoretical and practical level. First, the theory. Referring to the work of Friedrich Hayek, the father of much of this political philosophy, Plant shows how in the view of the Right 'questions of social justice can only arise when there is agency and intention'.[19] This means that those who grow poorer as a result of the *impersonal* mechanism of the market, i.e., those who find they are unable to compete well, are unable to sell their labour or goods or services and buy the goods and services of others — and this could be for a whole variety of reasons to do with their abilities, education, changing economic circumstances and needs etc — these people cannot be said to be suffering from injustice, even if at the end of the day through unemployment or low pay or whatever, they become very poor. It is just the lottery of the market . . . 'although they embody human actions, markets are much more like the weather in that their outcomes are not foreseen or intended. Hence those who end up with least, and suffer disadvantage, have not suffered an injustice and there is no justifiable claim that they can make on society for a rectification of their condition.'[20] (Reflecting his belief that social justice is an unattainable concept in a modern society, Hayek gives the second volume of his *Law, Legislation and Liberty*, the title *The Mirage of Social Justice*.[21])

In addition to such theoretical arguments, the New Right have a practical reason for welcoming inequality. In their view it encourages initiative and enterprise though this would seem to be more an article of faith than based on any hard empirical evidence. In his pamphlet, *The New Conservatism*, Nigel Lawson labels equality a false trail and a delusion; reflecting on the Conservative tradition particularly in the post war years, he comments: '. . . during the 25 years that followed Churchill it was a very different outlook that gained the intellectual ascendancy: the philosophy of social democracy with its profound faith in the efficiency of government action, particularly in the economic sphere, and its deep commitment to the notion of "equality". To a greater or lesser extent, the Conservative party embraced both these delusions. . . . The distinctive feature of the new Conservatism is its rejection of these false trails and its return to the mainstream.'[22]

A third key value that Plant highlights is *community*. As we have seen the New Right places heavy emphasis on the place of the individual at the expense of any understanding of society in terms of a common life together. Again, there are theoretical and practical reasons that lead them to be sceptical of this value: practically they are sceptical, because they see in community a value which is 'antagonistic to modernisation and economic progress'.[23] Theoretically they are sceptical because they believe that the idea of community presupposes shared ends and values which are just not there in a complex, modern, pluralist society such as ours. It would seem that the only way thinkers and politicians on the radical Right would embrace any understanding of community would be through clubs and associations that people voluntarily opt into, and private individual philanthropy, i.e. individual neighbourly care. Laying aside the effectiveness of this latter approach as a social policy, the overwhelming thrust of the ideology — the pursuit of private self-interest — would seem to contradict and undermine it.

Freedom, social justice and community. We need to be clear that in these three areas at least, the Right are working on quite fundamentally differing understandings and assumptions from very many Christians in an ideological approach that is underpinned by an apparently clear body of thought. Ideologies are of course, as Wogaman suggests, 'a complex weaving' and there are many other strands and outworkings. However hopefully enough has been said to attempt some kind of assessment. First, there are features of Laissez-faire Capitalism that Christians should welcome. For example, a free market *is* a much more efficient and responsive means of production and distribution — though only for those who can pay the price. Second, a free market does encourage the initiative and creativity of individuals and groups, thereby enhancing individual liberty and affirming humans as stewards of creation made in the image of the Creator God. Third, the state can indeed be very restrictive and coercive, as well as inefficient in terms of economic planning — though it can also be supportive. Despite the caveats, all these are broadly true. We need to recognise that the free market plays a crucially important economic and moral role in society. However, Christians have a special concern for the poor. How do they fare? How they are treated in any society is a kind of litmus test of the health of that society. Plant insists that 'it would be a travesty of their position [the New Right] to portray it as being unconcerned with the poor. They are concerned but in their view, ideas about social justice and equality stand in the way of an appreciation of the best mechanism for dealing with poverty, which is the free market. On their view the free market will bring about what is called for, either through the "echelon advance" or the "trickle down" mechanism, whereby what the rich consume today will gradually trickle down to the rest of society over time.'[24] In the third part of the Winchester paper, it is shown how the 'trickle down' effect is not working as defenders of the free market would hope, and a more recent briefing paper produced by the Low Pay Unit and Child Poverty Action Group entitled 'An Abundance of Poverty'[25] amply bears this out.

The Winchester paper tries to give a fair account of the Conservative capitalist position. Others are less willing to give the tag of moral respectability to an ideological tendency which stripped of its philosophical garb appears as naked selfish greed — 'possessive individualism'.[26] 'By your fruits shall you know them,' said Jesus. What are the results? After more than ten years of a government of this tendency, while there has been increased wealth for some — perhaps the majority — in terms of the overall social fabric of the community of the nation, it would seem that they are very serious indeed: by every measurement, we now live in a society that is markedly less equal and more divided, with less freedom for the poor; a society with less sense of social justice, that knows increasing violence and crime, experiences a more authoritarian state, and is developing a social climate which appears to be hell-bent on material gratification at the cost of other values.

It is easy to despair. It is also easy, and very tempting to put the blame solely at the door of the government of the last ten years. It may be though, that what we have seen in the last decade is simply the more aggressive,, no holds barred pursuit of a potentially destructive ideology that was there all the time embedded deeply in our culture, though before in various ways masked, softened, and ameliorated. Perhaps we have been for a long time, more sick than we know — a sickness of the culture, of the collective soul? We are back to Merton. And yet there is a connection between the sickness that he exposed, and the values of this ideology: for the frenetic flight away from the contemplative values that he pointed to — 'values which we fear' — would seem to find their full-blown centrifugal out-working in the crude and aggressive culture that increasingly engulfs us. It is the positive encouragement of *unrestrained* Capitalism that has been the particularly damning feature of the New Right.

However, clearly the sickness is more deep rooted. In his book *The Cultural Contradictions of Capitalism*, Professor Daniel Bell, writing of the United States — though the analysis is appropriate for Britain too — shows how capitalism which was founded on values which emphasise work, thrift, sobriety, honesty, frugality, self-control etc, derived from the 'Protestant ethic' and the 'Puritan temper',[27] has degenerated during the twentieth century into a morally vacuous hedonism — the pursuit of pleasure for its own sake. Bell's main point spelt out in his title is that in this process the economic system of capitalism with its emphasis now on spending and instant gratification, has undermined its own traditional value base — eaten away its own moral foundations — and thus lost its 'traditional legitimacy'.[28] This is the cultural contradiction of capitalism. What we are seeing in the latter half of this century is the destruction of those values that have both *sustained* capitalism and *restrained* it. Personal values such as hard work, thrift and honesty, acted both as a *spur* to capitalist enterprise leading men — and it would have almost always been men — to be innovative, industrious, creative, frugal, hard-working etc and at the same time, by its strong moral ethic enshrined in such values as sobriety, frugality and self-control, there was a *restraint* on the development of an excessive, morally weakening, less disciplined life-style and social climate. Gradually however, the power of those puritan values has been eroded causing society to degenerate into the instant gratification-of-all-wants mayhem, that now surrounds us. And, Bell's point is, this has been through the *very success of capitalism itself*. The result is that '. . . the social order lacks either a culture that is a symbolic expression of any vitality or a moral impulse that is a motivational or binding force. What, then, can hold society together?'[29] In this situation and crisis where the problems are of 'the kind of meanings that sustain a society', Bell risks an 'unfashionable answer — the return in western society of some conception of religion.'[30] Without a sense of 'the sacred', we are left with 'the shambles of appetite and self-interest and the destruction of the moral circle which engirds mankind.'[31]

Bell writes as an American of a deposit — which he believes is now exhausted — of personal and community values which gave vitality to a culture, helped create a more responsible social climate, and set clear limits. While we may have doubts about the attractiveness of such puritan values, and might wish to point out the dark and repressive side that distorted and prevented the emergence of a fuller humanity, it does seem that they, and the religious understandings that undergirded them, at least gave a moral dynamism and strength to a culture, that is now fast ebbing. It is, no doubt, the recognition of this that has led to a call for a return to 'Victorian values'. But the irony is that this call is coming from those who, at the very same time, by their encouragement of consumer materialism are undermining those very values that they are calling for. Perhaps the clearest example of this contradiction is in the area of family life, and the values such as loyalty, perseverance and commitment, that are needed to sustain it. These values are central in the marriage service where the promise is 'for better or worse, for richer or poorer, in sickness and in health . . .' Christopher Lasch, the American social theorist writes: '. . . the logic of consumerism . . . undermines the values of loyalty and perseverance and promotes a different set of values that are destructive of family life. The need for novelty and fresh stimulation becomes ever more intense, intervening interludes of boredom are increasingly intolerable.'[32]

Our culture then, in so far as we have embraced the creed of consumer capitalism, is a culture eating away its own moral foundations as well as being divided against itself. In Britain there remains a strong traditionalist streak within the Conservative Party which sees a role for the state in trying to uphold traditional values, but while there are occasional victories such as the vote against sunday trading, it is ineffective and puny against the overwhelming thrust of the *economic* ideology.

Symptomatic also of this moral confusion and contradiction is an alarming lack of social vision. Bell's question, 'what can hold society together?', is crucial, but, as he suggests, a moral impulse is required that is more than just a *binding* force. Motivation, vision, purpose *beyond* ourselves is required that will offer more than just social glue. 'Without a vision the people perish' (Prov 29:18). The more important question is: 'who or what are we living *for*.' The reality of a world of mass starvation and suffering, as well as the growing poverty in our own midst, presses this question ever more urgently upon us, even as privately we consume more. Which Christian has not felt the force of such tensions? The need for a vision that takes us beyond our own narrow self-interest is urgent.

Another study, much quoted, which underlines the deep rooted nature of our social malaise is Alasdair MacIntyre's *After Virtue* published in 1981. However again, the symptoms of cultural sickness that MacIntyre identifies are above all the features of Laissez-faire Capitalism. Looking back to the civilised Greek tradition of 'The Virtues' he sees it as fundamentally at variance with 'central features of the modern economic order and more especially its individualism, its acquisitiveness, and its elevation of the values of the market to a central social place.'[33] His assessment is that our society, bearing these disfigurements, has no 'shared moral first principles' with the result that 'modern politics is civil war carried on by other means.'[34] Like Bell, MacIntyre also suggests a religious 'answer'. In the last paragraph of the book he writes suggestively: 'If the tradition of the Virtues was able to survive the horrors of the last dark ages, we are not entirely without grounds for hope. This time however the barbarians are not waiting beyond the frontiers; they have already been governing us for quite some time. And it is our lack of consciousness of this that constitutes part of our predicament. We are waiting not for a Godot, but for another — doubtless very different — St Benedict.'[35]

A Crisis of Legitimacy

The situation that MacIntyre highlights when he talks of 'no shared moral first principles' and Bell refers to as a problem of 'the kind of meanings that sustain a society,' Forrester earths as a *'crisis of legitimacy'*, which he sees as the fundamental crisis in our society: 'no longer is there a generally accepted criterion by reference to which value conflicts may be resolved and the social system validated.'[36] Forrester sees the emergence of the New Right and the shattering of the cross-party consensus on values and goals as a key moment when a void was opened up and the crisis precipitated. In order to undergird their ideology, the New Right, in both Britain and the United States, vigorously claim a religious legitimacy; they look to the churches to provide this moral basis — the reassertion of traditional values of individual responsibility, family life and personal morality, and they are angry when the churches point to economic and social policy being among the chief causes for the corrosion of these very values. Hence the bad-tempered and fragile relationship between Church and state in Britain. Meanwhile the crisis of legitimacy remains with a resulting increase in conflict, for in championing the unrestrained market, in brushing aside any serious commitment to the common good, and in the failure to build and affirm any overall social consensus, by default, inner conflict and competitiveness have become *the* way of life for our society. Barbaric indeed.

From this basic 'crisis of legitimacy', there flows a second crisis — of *institutions*; the undermining of trust and confidence in such institutions as the police, parliament and the trades unions who cannot function effectively and with consent without a common value base. 'For a significant section of the population, the old loyalties to trade unions and political parties are not as firm as once they were, the parliamentary process is not treated with such respect, and the police are not seen as impartial. Trust in major social institutions is markedly eroded, and large groups like the unemployed, ethnic minorities or striking coal miners feel themselves marginalised and forgotten. No one of significance they feel, really listens to them, their voice is not heard.'[37]

The third crisis that Forrester identifies is a *crisis of community*. With growing inequalities, an erosion of trust in institutions, and the breakdown of a common value base, there follows an accelerated slide into lawlessness and crime leading to the steady disintegration of that value that is central to Christians — 'fellowship' or *koinonia* — what Lesslie Newbiggin calls 'one-anotherness'.[38]

In this situation what is demanded of us? Christians are involved in response with others of different faiths and none, in an enormous variety of ways. I have mentioned some above. The church too has a primary responsibility for the nourishing of its own community life — what David Jenkins referred to in his Hibbert lecture as, the building up of 'communities of endurance around a celebration of the Gospel of the God who is committed to our world, our society and our future for the sake of his Kingdom.'[39] MacIntyre similarly stresses the importance of constructing 'local forms of community within which civility and the intellectual and moral life can be sustained through the new dark ages which are already upon us.'[40] But what is meant here is not a network of isolated communities nourishing light and warmth for themselves in the midst of growing violence and despair. The search for the Kingdom always pushes us outwards towards the seeking with others of a basis for an alternative social vision.

Doctrines that drive us to Politics

What is required is a clearer *political* theology for our 'today' — the 'exploration, sustaining and commending of a Christian social vision'.[41] The situation is serious. A moral vacuum underlies much modern politics which helps to explain its strident tone. What are the resources that can be brought to bear from the tradition of Christian thought about God? Are there, to use David Jenkin's phrase, 'doctrines that drive One to politics'[42] and if so, how do they work? We are back to the earlier question: how does Christian belief about God and his purposes inform our values and so provide guidance towards the kind of ideology that we can say yes to, and help to shape, and the kind of ideology that we must say no to, and oppose? That is where the search is leading. In this study we are in search of the Kingdom, and the Kingdom while being as the New Testament makes clear, a radical eschatological reversal of all worldly values, is *also* the more humdrum collecting of building blocks that will form the foundation for politically feasible structures here and now, structures that will not bring in Utopia but will ensure a measure of justice and peace for *all*. We are then in search of a basis in the Christian tradition for values from which policy should flow, and against which policy should be judged.

Building blocks for the Kingdom. But first three clarifications. First, what is possible in the making of this connection between faith and politics? In one sense, everything. 'The world' Paul triumphantly exclaimed to the Corinthians, '. . . life and death, the present and the future, are all your servants, but you belong to Christ, and Christ to God' (1 Cor 3:25). Faith believes everything, shifts mountains, expects mustard trees to bloom! But in another sense, faith will demand hard realism. There is no blueprint in the Bible or anywhere else for a Christian society. Doctrines may drive us to politics, but they cannot prescribe politics in any detail. 'The movement from Christian revelation to political action isn't direct. It depends on technical and practical judgements about the actual situation and available political alternatives.'[43]

Second, we need to try to grasp that doctrines are truths *lived*, not simply learnt, as the story of Thomas Merton makes painfully and joyfully clear. The Protestant notion of first understanding and then living out truth in some kind of neat rational sequence needs to be stood on its head. Faith rather must go in search of understanding. The truth will only be discovered, grasped, stumbled upon, as it is lived, riskily, into the future in the very particular situations where we find ourselves. Doctrines, like the Kingdom itself, are elusive, we need to go in search of their meaning through our lives and community organisations — and somehow that meaning will always be on the other side of a cross.

Third, we need to recognise that even then, doctrines will serve as inadequate, provisional pointers to the Life of God which is beyond all doctrine. There can be no final statement of fulfilment of God's purposes for society. He is the *God of Surprises*,[44] the God of Abraham, always beckoning the human project into the future, enlarging and extending the vision and the promise of the Kingdom. We will never have it wrapped up. The Kingdom, though here and now, is fundamentally an eschatological symbol, i.e. it will only be fully realised at the end of history — the *eschaton*. Then and only then will the poor fully receive the Kingdom; then and only then will the gentle be/given the earth for their possession; then and only then will those who mourn all be comforted; then and only then will those who hunger and thirst to see right prevail, at last be satisfied. . . So the Kingdom acts as both yeast — leavening power *within* history — and judgement from the end, *upon* history. Up until that 'end', that 'then', we live in the tension between the now and the not yet, with doctrines and sacraments as inadequate signs pointing *forward*. But this must be cause for the politics of hope, never a recipe for the politics of resignation.

How then do the doctrines that drive us to politics actually work? Building blocks is perhaps an unfortunate, heavy and static image. Think rather of Jesus' dynamic picture of yeast leavening flattened dough. It is what the French poet and visionary Charles Péguy called 'mystique' — 'nothing less than the conjunction of the spirit of God at work in the world with the activities of men in the founding and practice of their institutions. It is essentially active, the working of leaven in the meal.'[45] Forrester summarises what 'mystique' provides under three headings: '(a) a shared vision, common goals, the underlying degree of value consensus which is necessary for healthy community life; (b) a powerful source of motivation for relatively disinterested and imaginative work in the civil community; (c) an effective sustaining force for those who bear the burden of taking difficult decisions which affect the destiny of others.'[46]

A shared vision, a source of motivation, a sustaining force. The implication is of something dynamic, potent. As we examine, discuss and preach about the classic Christian doctrines, in our eagerness to make them tidy and logical there is a constant danger of robbing them of this potent 'mystique'. Just as, in this search we do not, like Abraham, know where we are going; so we might as well acknowledge that much of the time, with Christian doctrine, we do not know what we are talking about. But if God really is who the Bible says he is, then the doctrines of God will fundamentally question all conventional political and economic thinking and raise up the promise of an infinitely more gentle world, redolent of the vision of the prophets. And if the Church was more rooted in these teachings, instead of living just a little uncomfortably alongside and in the values of our culture, it would be far more often, appalled and anguished and angry, as well as actively engaged in the pursuit of something better. Doctrines, as we have said are inadequate pointers to God, but they are about *God*, and so must be of ultimate concern, determinative for us in every sphere of human activity. They need to be taken and carried out of the creeds and the churches, where isolated and separate, they are literally of no earthly use, and placed in the situations where political, economic, community and personal decisions are made — into the dough of the world, where the yeast, the 'mystique', can do its potent work.

Vision . . .

As we allow these classic Christian formulations — the doctrine of the Trinity, of Creation, Incarnation, the King-dom of God etc — to percolate deeply into our conscious-ness in the life of the Church, exposing truth and yielding meaning for our society, what direction do they begin to point us in? At this point, I simply want to suggest by way of example, the kind of insight Christian truth may reveal. First it might, for example, become alarmingly clear to us that an ideology which applauds, sanctions and encourages the aggressive and unrestrained pursuit of individual self-interest, and enshrines at its heart the competitive and divisive values of the market setting them up as determinat-ive in more and more aspects of life so that there is, in truth, very little society left, but only competing individuals and families, is an ideology which flies in the face of God as *Trinity* — 'the glory of love forever poured out and forever shared'[47] where the supreme value is self-giving love in a community of perpetual giving and receiving — 'a plurality of persons whose equality of dignity and mutuality of love present themselves as the pattern upon which human life could, and indeed must be shaped.'[48] An ideol-ogy that flies in the face of such a truth must ultimately be blasphemy. Work needs to be done in exploring the implications of this truth: what does it suggest about how we structure our Church life? What kind of political think-ing does it prompt? To this we shall come briefly in a moment. They are difficult questions, but they do not offset the uncomfortable fact that this foundational Christian understanding must fundamentally call in question the individualist thrust of this ideology.

Secondly, by way of example, we might see more clearly that an ideology which talks about freedom simply in nega-tive terms as 'the absence of coercion', declares that 'pov-erty is not unfreedom', and increasingly denies to poor people the resources for effective participation in the life of society, has not touched the earth where most people live, and so flies in the face of the principle of the *Incarnation* which insists that the material, i.e. matter and flesh, is the means through which the transcendent God works, and so demands that all policy be thought through and judged in terms of the enfleshed, material needs of *all*. Again this begs searching questions. What do we mean by 'freedom'? What positive economic and social rights — for example in the area of employment, health care, housing and education — should undergird the concept of freedom? How should 'needs' in a modern society such as ours be defined? To work at such questions is to give substance to the *principle* of the Incarnation, which insists on understanding freedom and responses to poverty, in terms of enfleshed, material existence.

Thirdly, we might begin to see more clearly that a devotion to free market principles is becoming a kind of idolatry if it insists that the market should determine the distribution of resources in such areas as health care and education, above the needs of humans. This is to fly in the face of the *Kingdom of God* as we know it from the teaching of Jesus, where life is the good gift of the Creator, given to all irrespective of desert, or moral worth, or ability, the Kingdom where all are of equal and infinite value in the eyes of the Giver. Crucial questions here are: what is meant by 'equality'? And how can this grace of the Kingdom for all practically be ensured? This would suggest the idea of a basic income, or social wage. The radical dissonance between this economic order and the teaching of Jesus impels us into such questions.

Fourthly, in this brief list of examples, it might come home more forcefully that an economic system — a system so often blind to the 'values inherent in living nature'[49] — that is built on the assumption of an infinite supply of raw materials that can be exploited and ripped from the earth to build up the life-styles of the rich in the first world, ultimately flies in the face of God as *Creator*, Preserver and Sustainer of the planet itself. The doctrine of Creation particularly suggests that Christians will be involved in the search for 'green' alternatives.

However, this mix of religion and politics is a heady and

dangerous thing. So lastly one more doctrine. The doctrine of *Original Sin* acts as a sharp and sobering brake on all utopian tendencies in politics, reminding us that no perfect political order can ever be ushered in, and to try to do so is to invite totalitarianism. This doctrine invites us to tread a hard realistic path between the politics of the left which understresses sin and believes that simply by the alteration of social structures the perfect society can be ushered in, and the politics of the right which overstresses sin and uses it as an excuse for inactivity in corporate involvement. Christian truth acknowledges both tendencies but goes further and insists: the world is fundamentally *good*, is *also* fallen and corrupt, *but* has been redeemed! All three are and will remain true, and so demand of us hopeful realistic attention to the nitty-gritty realities of every situation, respecting human freedom.

... and a Principle: Koinonia

Trinity, Incarnation, Kingdom of God, Creation, Original Sin. Five classic Christian doctrines that are suggestive and potent for Christian thinking about the shape and possibilities of our politics. However, though potent, the way these doctrines work would suggest that they are limited — suggestive and directive only. Despite the caution expressed earlier about doctrines prescribing politics, we need to ask, can we say more? Does the Christian tradition offer some kind of overall *prescriptive principle?* The report 'Changing Britain' from the Anglican Board for Social Responsibility suggests that in the concept of *koinonia*, such a prescriptive principle, which can be applied to all levels of society, is indeed available to us.

Koinonia is a 'Greek word . . . used in early Christian writings to signify a relation between persons resulting from their participation in one and the same reality.'[50] Within the life of the Church, it is often translated as 'fellowship' or 'communion' but neither of these is satisfactory nor able to comprehend the range of meaning that *koinonia* tries to express. In the New Testament the basis of *koinonia* is the ultimate reality of God the Trinity — the life of God as Father, known through Jesus Christ, and experienced in the present through the Spirit. This gives *koinonia* its fullest meaning. *Koinonia* stresses that we shall find fulfilment neither in individual freedom, nor in absorbtion or submersion in a community, but rather in a dynamic tension of the two polarities: *koinonia* therefore means *persons-in-community* and leads to the concept of *interdependence* in social relations.

Perhaps this principle becomes clearest to us in and through the life of the family. Every family where there is human flourishing will know the importance of encouraging individual freedom and self-expression. But it is a freedom nurtured in the security and belonging of a shared life together expressed through meals, play, routines, rituals etc. Both poles are important. Overstress individuality — I shall do what I want at my time and convenience — and the family degenerates and disintegrates into a collection of individuals at war; no nourishment, no mutual affirmation, affection withers and trust is eroded, as each is for himself or herself alone. Overstress community — belonging together — and the family becomes a breathless suffocating cocoon to be escaped from. The flourishing is found in the dynamic tension between the two. *Koinonia* holds them together.

However, with a high divorce rate and growing numbers of single parent households, 'the family' may be a most unhelpful model to choose to illustrate *koinonia* — and in a sense inappropriate too, for the whole point of *koinonia* in the New Testament is that it expresses a bond which goes *beyond* and may be far deeper than the ties of blood relationships. *Koinonia* is the establishment of a new community across the boundaries of family, tribe, ethnic group, social class, nation. As Paul wrote to the Galatians, we are all 'one in Christ Jesus' (Gal 3:28).

A better illustration of what is meant by *koinonia* is through the approach of Community Development — a way of working with local neighbourhoods, particularly in poorer areas, which the church is increasingly becoming involved in. In so far as Community Development, (*a*) searches with people in a particular neighbourhood for a common basis for shared concerns (and the concerns will often be very mundane, for example, anxiety or anger over bad housing, or lack of play space for children), (*b*) works to hold together groups and build trust, drawing out the skills and contributions of individuals and (*c*) seeks to encourage people *together* to take power to change their community and circumstances by discovering and pressing for those resources that they need, it is a method of working which is a living expression of *koinonia*. One of the main recommendations of *Faith in the City*, the Archbishop's Commission on Urban Priority Areas, was that Dioceses of the Church of England should become involved in developing and supporting Community Development projects.[51] It is a powerful means of extending the understanding of *koinonia* into the life of the community at local level.

This New Testament principle, rooted in the very life of God Himself, offers the undergirding principle, beyond the life of the church, for society itself. 'The concept of *koinonia* and the range of reflections prompted by it challenges all social agencies — cultural, political and economic — to balance many values together . . . Churches have a duty to society, not just to themselves, to work at this vision and communicate in word and deed, and to witness to the source of all these values in God.'[52] It acts too as a kind of touchstone helping us to judge between ideologies and specific policies, and suggests a hard to tread political middle path between on the one hand, unrestrained individualism, and on the other hand, restrictive collectivism, and leads us towards the ideologies of social market capitalism or democratic socialism as being legitimate options for Christians to go for, and to back, in terms of political support in our particular society. In that they seek to affirm the freedom of the individual within social structures and institutions that guard and enhance common values, these are the ideological frameworks in our kind of society within which Christians may hear faint echoes of their own understandings about ultimate reality — though they will often be very faint!

There will be many other factors related to Christian discipleship which should inform our political choices, but *koinonia* would seem to be a key principle. In *Faith in the Nation* John Atherton has developed a Christian social vision for Britain which he calls a 'Participating and Reciprocal Society'.[53] It is based on the twin doctrines of the Body of Christ and 'the Common Good' both of which find liturgical expression at the heart of the Eucharist. Both are themselves expressions of the doctrine of *koinonia* — persons-in-community. I refer the reader to his work as an important contribution to this discussion.

In this work of seeking a basis for Christian social vision — seeking the meaning of the Kingdom in society — there is a lot of hard thinking to be done. We cannot merely try to grasp broad understandings of a few doctrines and basic principles and hope that is enough. 'The Church' writes Atherton, 'has to learn to think harder, and in more detail, and more comprehensively than ever before.'[54] In our present predicament, there is a particular challenge to Christian people to get more involved in the political debate at every level.

However this business of God and politics is not easy. There is the constant danger of confusing the radical other-worldly Kingdom of God which fundamentally questions all our values and structures and politics, with a set of very this-worldly limited political prescriptions. God is not to be identified with the Labour Party or indeed the Social and Liberal Democrats! The danger of such a confusion exists, and we need to be alert to it, but better to risk that confusion than not to get involved at all. For the Hebrew, it was in the process of history and political events that God revealed himself. Faithful discipleship then calls us to become involved, and far more than just thinking will be required. But the Kingdom is God's not ours. Attempts to be faithful to the Kingdom must be illuminated and nurtured in the warmth of a shared life of worship, a life where *koinonia* is *experienced* and becomes living doctrine, where we know we are indeed part of the Body of Christ, where we seek a common good amongst ourselves and beyond ourselves, where each lives for all and all for each. I have written much of this chapter while staying in a Franciscan friary. Such religious communities may seem remote from the lives of most of us, but in their common daily eucharistic life, where individuality is not submerged but enhanced, they do offer a striking model of *koinonia*. The meaning of such a doctrine only comes home to the heart as it is lived in families and in communities whether they be of a specifically religious nature or those less structured community groupings and associations to be found and built in local neighbourhoods, or in the life of the ordinary local Church where we must surely find ways of belonging more deeply together — bearing one another's burdens. As concern grows, it will be the love of God and the grace of God, experienced in and through one another, which will sufficiently give us the *courage* to get involved in politics at all, the *humility* to constantly question all we are doing, and the *vision* to enkindle the heart and mind of a nation far from God. We have a long way to go.

Perhaps in this particular part of the search we have hardly begun. The trouble, I suspect, is that many of us in our hearts still half believe that religion and politics don't and shouldn't mix; that God has nothing really to do with the world; and that religion is indeed as Edward Norman suggested 'the evocation of the unearthly'.[55] We cling to our private interior spiritualities — it feels so much more comfortable that way — for us who have the resources. There is an urgent task of theological *education* and, more important, theological *experience* here. What we are struggling with is surely nothing less than God Himself; either we respond to Him, love Him, serve Him, and walk in his ways, and so find that deep peace of belonging which the Jews called *Shalom;* or we assert our proud individual independence, turning our back on the poor in our own midst and beyond our shores, and so fly in his face, and therefore invite upon ourselves dislocation, violence and disaster. At the end of the day there is that simple choice.

Conclusion

In this search for the meaning of the Kingdom in and beyond our society, we have identified responses of personal support, social action, and engagement with specific issues leading into the questioning of ideology and politics. We have touched on the potent shaping power of Christian doctrine and have been led to the concept of *koinonia* as that which offers a principle against which we may test all political thinking. The task of filling out the meaning of this principle in every situation is demanding, and it will always be tempting to limit religion to some kind of narrow personal sphere. Above all, the work of contributing to the building of an alternative social vision does seem urgent. What is becoming more obvious every day is that there is an alarming void and vacuum in the area of social morality, and a consequent steady worsening in the degree of conflict, bewilderment, dislocation and suffering. Those in power have few answers that offer any hope at all. The churches have a crucial role to play. The novelist Iris Murdoch has written: 'There is a serious and growing void in our thinking about moral and social problems. This void is uneasily felt by society at large and is the more distressing since we are now perhaps for the first time in our history feeling the loss of religion as a consolation and a guide . . . A religious and moral vocabulary is the possession of a few; and most people lack the words with which to say just what is felt to be wrong . . .'[56]

The challenge to the Church is profound. Not only do we claim an ultimate consolation and an ultimate guide, but we also claim a religious and moral vocabulary which is both able to identify what is wrong, and is able to offer a vision of what could be, based on the life of the Word made flesh who dwelt among us. In other words we have a vocabulary that spells *hope*, but we seem so hesitant and afraid of exploring the meaning of that hope and articulating it more clearly to a society so clearly adrift.

But it will be spoken best through who we *are*. 'Use words — if you must' said St Francis to his brother friars when he sent them out on their mission. Finally, and briefly, we turn to some hesitant thoughts on the Church. It can hardly be excluded in any search for the Kingdom.

Epilogue: A Church in Search

'We do not know what to do, but our eyes are upon you'
(2 Chron 20:12)

In the last chapter, as we looked at the kind of political area that the search for the Kingdom may take us into, a central value that kept recurring is *community*, or to use the technical New Testament word, *koinonia*, which means 'persons-in-community'. Set against this it becomes clear that it is in its commitment to *individualism* that so much modern politics is so deeply flawed and at odds with the purposes of God and the deepest needs and patterning of our lives. Christian truth asserts that we cannot be made whole *alone* — we belong to each other, though we shall only find each other, in God. If then life in community is fundamental to human flourishing the search must lead us right into the life of the Church — into the *common* life of the Body of Christ.

This study has suggested that the hope and the promise of that *common* life — a sign of the Kingdom here and now — will be given, as we search in three areas particularly: in the biblical tradition and the teachings of the Church; in the life of prayer and spiritual direction; and in the questions of values and meanings as well as the practice of community building in the social and political life of society. As we have seen, none of these can be considered alone, each inter-relates with the other two, and all are about change. And all three need to be pursued in and by the community of the Church so that insights gained can be ploughed back into the very life of the Church, enriching and transforming it.

To what extent is this happening? To what extent does the Church at all levels of its life, take this search for the

Kingdom seriously? To what extent is there a commitment to digging with all the analytical tools of modern scholarship into the tradition of faith? How concerned are we for a deepening of the ministry of spiritual direction and the encouragement of the contemplative way? How committed are we to seeking the values and life of the Kingdom in our society and local community?

Hard questions — though the answers are surely not all negative? However, it does seem that in two of these areas, there is serious weakness. In his book, *Beyond Decline: a challenge to the churches*, Robin Gill who is both a university lecturer in Christian ethics and a parish priest, suggests that in two of these areas, theology and social involvement, the churches are not thinking hard enough. In the first area, he identifies a serious 'Gulf between Theory and Practice' and 'a disastrous anti-intellectualism in the British churches . . .'[1] With regard to the second area, he identifies a 'Gulf in Social Pronouncements' whereby the churches, in their doubt that they can any longer be a central source for moral values in a pluralist society, are tempted continually to espouse and lobby for specific partisan causes and issues.[2] He sees the radicals putting pressure on Church Assemblies and Synods — as the official church bodies — constantly to make pronouncements on a wide range of social issues without sufficient regard for constraints, consensus and what is possible. This creates a strong reaction in a conservative group which wants to stop churches engaging in any moral and social issues and concentrate instead upon 'the gospel'. The result is that it is not just politics that is civil war carried on by other means. Gill believes that the churches should be involved in social issues, but not necessarily in this way — through official pronouncements. He offers his own five ways whereby 'Christians in a pluralist society can engage effectively in moral and social issues'.[3] They are: individual prophecy; group prophecy (he gives the example of Christian CND); sectarian prophecy — a response to a society which is perceived to be evil (the example is the South African 'Kairos' Document); transposition of Christian values —

this has been the particular focus in the previous chapter; and moral praxis — practical love in action, for example over the issues of AIDS. In addition to specific pieces of prophecy and practice, we need to note too that many Christians, in the course of their everyday working life, will have opportunity to engage effectively in moral and social issues, and the Church community needs to recognise and resource them in this.

In these two areas of theology and social involvement, it would seem that more careful thought needs to be given. Whether or not there is a similar failure to reflect and engage deeply in the second area — the work of encouraging spiritual direction and a contemplation that nourishes action and vision — is perhaps more questionable, as there is clearly an enormous amount of interest in this area — witness the continuing sale of books by Thomas Merton.

Whatever current strengths and weaknesses there may be, the question needs to be pressed: are these concerns — for theology, for contemplative prayer, and for social engagement — central and determinative for the Church in its understanding of mission and ministry? Or are they, while theoretically assented to, and acknowledged by all to be important, in actual fact treated as marginal and peripheral, crowded out by the all-consuming questions of Church government and maintenance? It is as always, a question of priorities. How do we use our God given time within the community life of the Church? Do we regularly and as a priority make room for theological discussion and sharing, drawing on academic insight, the development of contemplative spirituality, and exploration into issues of social engagement leading to action with others, in addition to, or perhaps instead of, our preoccupations with survival, maintenance and numbers?

If it is right that these three areas must be priorities, the challenge is for the Church at every level to find ways of deepening its understanding and practice of all of them. This must involve at the very least: a greater emphasis on the training and sharing together of the whole people of God; closer contact with specialist centres, for example, universities, hospitals and counselling centres, as well as contact with pieces of good community work practice; the using and developing of its own institutions (for example The William Temple Foundation): and, flowing from all this, the search for different approaches to ministry in different situations — urban, rural and suburban.

Perhaps what is required just seems too daunting. But we have been given the searching Spirit. We have only to begin — perhaps with the help of those more experienced in all these areas — where we are: with the issues of our local community, with our own stumbling attempts at praying, with our particular faith understandings. Where is the Kingdom here — in this place? In *Praying the Kingdom*, Charles Elliott recounts how Bishop Stephen Verney 'set himself the task of sitting down with every church council in the diocese and asking each one; "What is God doing here and now?" Some told him it was an improper, even indecent question. "You can't expect God to be *here* — not *now* . . ." That seldom lasted. Slowly, after time for reflection, people began to share amazing insights of grace at work in individuals, groups, whole communities. . . . It was clear that for many it was the first time they had thought of it in that way . . . and what a joyful discovery it was for them! Perhaps, after all, God was alive and living amongst them.'[4]

God alive — and living amongst us. It is in the quality of our common life, our *koinonia*, that the Kingdom will be most clearly glimpsed both by ourselves and others, a quality of self-giving love discovered together as we go, as the pilgrim people of God, nourished by Christ in the Eucharist, in search of the Kingdom which is always beyond us, and adhere to some kind of recognisable common life discovering different values from the society around.

In this going in search, perhaps one particular quality is more important than all else: ignorance — or 'unknowing'. The way to the Kingdom requires that we get into the way of it — that we develop a kind of holy and child-like ignorance that is not naivety, but openness — openness to God and the future. The Kingdom always demands a stripping down, an abandonment of the familiar, and a waiting . . .

At the end of another search book — the account by Gerard Hughes of his walk from Weybridge to Rome entitled *In Search of a Way*[5] — Hughes makes this 'ignorance' the focus of a prayer — a prayer for the Kingdom. I would like to end this book too with that prayer which I have adapted a little, for it sums up better than anything else, that which I have tried here to comprehend:

Lord save us from every form of certainty which can rob us of this precious ignorance. Help us to keep searching after you, in our lives and in our world, and not to cease from searching until we reach the end of the pilgrimage when every tear will be wiped away and we shall know you, our God, as you are, and in you finally be entirely at one, with ourselves, with all men and women, and with all creation.

References

Introduction

1. Paul Tillich, *The Shaking of the Foundations* (SCM Press, 1949) Ch. 7.
2. Simeon Nkoane, *Spirituality in a Violent Society*, Eric Symes Abbot Memorial Lecture, King's College London, May 1987, (published by Southwell and Oxford Papers on Contemporary Society — Sept 1987).
3. Eric James, *The Life of J. A. T. Robinson, Scholar, Pastor and Prophet* (Collins, 1987) p 136.

Chapter 1: A People in Search

1. Kenneth Leech, *True God* (Sheldon Press, 1985) pp 70–71.
2. Jürgen Moltmann, *On Human Dignity* (SCM Press, 1984) p 192.
3. *Ibid* p 203.
4. Lionel Blue, *To Heaven with Scribes and Pharisees* (DLT, 1975) p 10.
5. Gerhard von Rad, *Genesis* (SCM Press, Old Testament Library 1961) p 183.
6. Jürgen Moltmann, *Theology of Hope* (SCM Press, 1967) p 141.
7. See the discussion about the meaning of the Divine Name in Bernhard W. Anderson, *The Living World of the Old Testament* (Longman, 1958) p 55.
8. Martin Buber, *The Prophetic Faith* pp 208 ff, cited in *The Living World of the Old Testament* p 445.
9. Claus Westermann, *Isaiah 40–66* (SCM Press, Old Testament Library 1969) p 425.
10. Alan Ecclestone, *The Night Sky of the Lord* (DLT, 1980) p 37.
11. Norman Perrin, *Jesus and the Language of the Kingdom* (SCM Press, 1976) p 26.
12. *Ibid.* p 28.

Chapter 2: The Heart of the Search

1. For this brief summary of these four groupings, I am much indebted to Hans Ruedi-Weber, *Experiments with Bible Study* (World Council of Churches, 1981) Ch. 14. Also see Gerd Theissen, *The Shadow of the Galilean* (SCM Press, 1987) for a most illuminating account, in narrative form, of the world of Jesus' day.
2. *Ibid.* p 172.
3. *Ibid.* p 173.
4. *Ibid.* p 172.
5. Joachim Jeremias, *New Testament Theology Volume 1.* (SCM Press, 1971) p 29.
6. C. H. Dodd, *The Founder of Christianity* (Collins, 1971)
7. Edward Schillebeecx, *Jesus, an experiment in Christology* (Collins, 1979) p 156.
8. James P. Mackey, *Jesus, the Man and the Myth* (SCM Press, 1979) Ch. 4. Also see James P. Mackey, *Modern Theology: A Sense of Direction* (Oxford University Press, 1987) particularly for the discussion on the Eucharist in Ch. 3.
9. *Ibid.* p 134.
10. *Ibid.* p 134.
11. Jeremias, *New Testament Theology Vol. 1. op. cit.* p 115 (footnote 2).
12. *Ibid.* p 115.
13. Mackey, *Jesus, the Man and the Myth op. cit.* pp 148–9.
14. Schillebeeckx *Jesus, an experiment in Christology op. cit.* p 184.

PART TWO

Chapter 3: The Personal Search

1. Paul Tillich, *The Boundaries of our Being* (Fontana, 1973) p 22.
2. Alan Jones, *Soul Making, The Desert Way of Spirituality* (SCM Press, 1986) p 164.
3. *Ibid.* p 171.
4. Quoted on the cover of the Sheldon Press Edition of *The Seven Storey Mountain* (Sheldon Press, 1975).
5. Thomas Merton writing in January 1967 to the writer of a thesis, quoted in Michael Mott, *The Seven Mountains of Thomas Merton* (Mifflin 1984, published in Britain by Sheldon Press 1986) Preface p xxvi.

Chapter 4: The Road to Eden

Almost all the quotations in this chapter are from *The Seven Storey Mountain* (Harcourt Brace Jovanovich Inc, 1948; Published in Britain by Sheldon Press, 1975). Where a page number is cited against a reference, it refers to the page in the Sheldon Press edition.

1. p 5.
2. p 8.
3. p 10.
4. p 11.
5. p 5.
6. p 14.
7. p 15.
8. p 32.
9. p 37.
10. p 49.
11. *Ibid.*
12. p 71.
13. p 101.
14. p 109.
15. p 108.
16. p 111.
17. p 118.
18. p 123.
19. p 124.
20. p 125.
21. p 127.
22. Monica Furlong, *Merton: A Biography* (Collins, 1980) p 60.
23. *Ibid. Introduction* pp xiv-xv.
24. p 127.
25. Thomas Merton, *Love and Living* (Sheldon Press, 1979) p 13.
26. p 157.
27. p 160.
28. p 164.
29. p 172.
30. p 175.
31. p 191.
32. p 207.
33. p 211.
34. p 224.
35. p 238.

36. p 248.
37. p 253.
38. p 226.
39. p 255.
40. p 296.
41. p 298.
42. p. 300.
43. p 320.
44. p 325.
45. p 325.
46. p 348.
47. p 364–5.
48. p 366.
49. p 368–9.
Reflection
50. p 284.
51. p 397.
52. p 412.
53. p 379.

Chapter 5: The Ruins of my Heart

Most of the quotations in this chapter are from Thomas Merton, *The Sign of Jonas* (Harcourt Brace and Co., 1953, published in Britain by Sheldon Press, 1976). Where a page number is cited against a reference it refers to the page in the Sheldon Press edition.

1. This very brief summary of life in the monastery is taken from the descriptions in Monica Furlong's and Michael Mott's biographies to which I am much indebted. For a fuller picture, I refer the reader to their work, particularly chapter 8 in Furlong 'Among the Shining Vineyards'; and Part 5 in Mott, 'Mount Purgatory'. I am also indebted to George Woodcock, *Thomas Merton, Monk and Poet, a critical study* (Canongate, 1978) Ch. 3, 'The Walls of Gethsemani' for the description of the setting of the monastery.
2. Merton, *The Seven Storey Mountain, op. cit.* p 421.
3. Andre Chastel, *The Age of Humanism* (London, Thames and Hudson 1962) cited in Mott, *The Seven Mountains of Thomas Merton, op. cit.* p 205.
4. Mott, *The Seven Mountains of Thomas Merton, op. cit.* p 208.

5. Thomas Merton, *Exile ends in Glory* (Milwaukee: Bruce 1948) cited in Furlong, *Merton: A Biography*, *op. cit.* p 124.

6. Furlong, *Merton: A Biography*, *op. cit.* pp 126–7.

7. Woodock, *Thomas Merton, Monk and Poet, a critical study*, *op. cit.* p 44.

8. Merton, *The Seven Storey Mountain*, *op. cit.* p 380.

9. p 32.

10. p 56.

11. p 30.

12. p 115.

13. Mott, *The Seven Mountains of Thomas Merton*, *op. cit.* p 205.

14. p 201.

15. p 321.

16. Thomas Merton, *The Seven Storey Mountain*, *op. cit.* p 191.

17. p 202.

18. Thomas Merton, *Conjectures of a Guilty Bystander* (Burns and Oates, 1968) p 117.

19. *Ibid.* pp 269–70.

20. p 181.

21. p 200.

22. p 225.

23. James Finlay, *Merton's Palace of Nowhere* (Ave Maria Press, 1978) p 17.

24. See particularly his essay 'Is the world a problem?' in *Contemplation in a World of Action* (Unwin, 1980) p 143 ff.

25. p 230.

26. p 251.

27. p 230.

28. p 238.

29. p 239.

30. p 240.

31. p 246.

32. p 249.

33. p 253.

34. p 254.

35. *Ibid.*

36. p 259.

37. Merton, *The Seven Storey Mountain*, *op. cit.* p 14.

38. Ibid., p 71.

39. pp 230–231.

40. p 325.

41. p 328.

42. p 330.
43. pp 322–3.
44. p 334.
Reflection
45. Merton, *The Seven Storey Mountain, op. cit.* p 422.
46. Jones, *Soul Making, the Desert Way of Spirituality, op. cit.* p 23.
47. Finlay, *Merton's Palace of Nowhere, op. cit.* p 151.
48. p 262.
49. p 230.
50. Jones, *Soul Making, the Desert Way of Spirituality, op. cit.*, p 174.
51. pp 230–1.
52. p 263.
53. p 254.
54. Tillich, *The Shaking of the Foundations, op. cit.* p 161.

Chapter 6 The Roots of Protest

1. Jones, *Soul Making, the Desert Way of Spirituality, op. cit.* p 171.
2. Thomas Merton, *Raids on the Unspeakable* (Burns and Oates, 1977) p 132.
3. Thomas Merton, *No Man is an Island* (Burns and Oates, 1955) Prologue p xv.
4. *Ibid.* pp xiv-xv.
5. Jones, *Soul Making, the Desert Way of Spirituality, op. cit.* p 181.
6. Merton, *Conjectures of a Guilty Bystander, op. cit.* pp 140–1.
7. Thomas Merton, *Contemplative Prayer* (DLT, 1973) p 25.
8. Furlong, *Merton: A Biography, op. cit.* p 178.
9. Thomas Merton, *The Ascent to Truth* (Burns and Oates, 1951) p 43.
10. *Ibid.* pp 220–1.
11. *Ibid.* p 38.
12. *Ibid.* p 39.
13. *Ibid.* p 221.
14. Thomas Merton, *Bread in the Wilderness* (Burns and Oates, 1954) pp 68–70.

15. Thomas Merton, *Seeds of Contemplation* (Anthony Clarke Books, 1972) pp 62–3.
16. Thomas Merton, *Contemplation in a World of Action, op. cit.* p 154.
17. Thomas Merton, *The Inner Experience: Notes on Contemplation* (unpublished) cited in Finlay, *Merton's Palace of Nowhere, op. cit.* p 91.
18. Merton, *Seeds of Contemplation, op. cit.* p 27.
19. Merton, *Conjectures of a Guilty Bystander, op. cit.* p 296.
20. Merton, *Contemplative Prayer, op. cit.* p 26.
21. Merton, *Conjectures of a Guilty Bystander, op. cit.* p 302.
22. Ibid. p 16.
23. Merton, *Raids on the Unspeakable, op. cit.* p 51.
24. Ibid. p 17.
25. Finlay, *Merton's Palace of Nowhere, op. cit.* p 26.
26. Merton, *Raids on the Unspeakable, op. cit.* p 16.
27. Merton, *Conjectures of a Guilty Bystander, op. cit.* p 169.
28. Thomas Merton, *On Peace* (Mowbrays, 1976) p 7 ff.
29. *Ibid.* p 82 ff.
30. Furlong, *Merton: A Biography, op. cit.* p 268.
31. Merton, *Conjectures of a Guilty Bystander, op. cit.* p 69.
32. See *The Asian Journal of Thomas Merton* (Sheldon Press, 1974)

Reflection

33. Merton, *Contemplative Prayer, op. cit*, from the Introduction by Douglas V. Steere.
34. Ecclestone, *The Night Sky of the Lord, op. cit.* pp 138, 146.
35. Christopher Fry, *A Sleep of Prisoners* (OUP, 1952) p 49. Cited in Alan Gawith, *The Church and Social Concern* (William Temple Foundation Occasional Paper No 12).
36. Patrick Hart (Editor) *Thomas Merton, Monk* (Hodder and Stoughton, 1975) from the chapter 'Man of Prayer' by David Steindl-Rast p 79.
37. *The Asian Journal of Thomas Merton, op. cit.* p 337.
38. *Ibid.* p 338.
39. Hart, *Thomas Merton, Monk, op. cit.* pp 80–81.

40. Margaret Hebblethwaite, *Motherhood and God* (Geoffrey Chapman, 1984) pp 110–1.

Chapter 7: A Question of Politics?

1. Board for Social Responsibility, Church House Dean's Yard, London SW1P 3NZ.
2. *Changing Britain* and *Not just for the Poor*, (Church House Publishing, Great Smith St, London SW1P 3NZ).
3. *The Church and the Bomb* (Church House Publishing, 1983).
4. *Faith in the City*, (Church House Publishing, 1985).
5. Eric James (editor), *God's Truth* (SCM Press, 1988) pp 36–37.
6. John Atherton, *Faith in the Nation* (SPCK, 1988) Ch. 5.
7. J. Philip Wogaman, *Christians and the Great Economic Debate* (SCM Press, 1977) pp 10, 12.
8. Duncan B. Forrester, *Theology and Politics* (Basil Blackwell, 1988) p 150.
9. Dietrich Bonhoeffer, *No Rusty Swords, Letters, Lectures and Notes 1928–1936* (London: Collins) p 161 f. Cited in Forrester, *Theology and Politics, op. cit.* p 170.
10. Ronald H. Preston, *The Future of Christian Ethics* (SCM Press, 1987) from the chapter 'The New Right: a Theological critique' p 135.
11. Keith Joseph and Jonathan Sumption, *Equality* (John Murray, 1979) p 48.
12. Ronald H. Preston, *Church and Society in the late Twentieth Century: the Economic and Political Task* (SCM Press, 1983) from the chapter 'The New Radical Right' p 65.
13. *Ibid.* p 66.
14. Peter Selby. *Liberating God, Private Care and Public Struggle* (SPCK, 1983) p 82.
15. Ludwig von Mises, *The Free and Prosperous Commonwealth: an exposition of the ideas of classical liberalism* (Princeton, New Jersey, van Nostrand Co., 1962) pp 88–89. Cited in Atherton, *Faith in the Nation, op. cit.* p 55.
16. Atherton, *Faith in the Nation, op. cit.* p 56.
17. *Faith in the City: Theological and Moral challenges* (Diocese of Winchester Church House, 9, The Close, Winchester, SO23 9LS) pp 12–13. For a fuller exploration of the ideology of the New Right, see K. Hoover and R. Plant, *Conservative Capitalism in Britain and the United States* (Routledge, 1988).
18. Joseph and Sumption, *Equality, op. cit.* p 47 ff.

19. *Faith in the City, op. cit.* p 7.
20. *Ibid.* p 8.
21. F. A. Hayek, *Law, Legislation and Liberty* (Routledge and Kegan Paul) (Vol. 1, 2 and 3 1973–1977) Cited in Footnote 3 of *Faith in the City: Theological and Moral Challenges, op. cit.* p 18.
22. Nigel Lawson, *The New Conservatism* (Centre for Policy Studies 8 Wilfred St, London SW1, 1980) p 2.
23. *Faith in the City: Theological and Moral Challenges, op. cit.* p 15.
24. *Ibid.* p 16.
25. Low Pay Unit and Child Poverty Action Group, *An Abundance of Poverty* 9 Upper Berkeley St, London W1H 8BY.
26. Preston, *Church and Society in the Late Twentieth Century, op. cit.* p 53.
27. Daniel Bell, *The Cultural Contradictions of Capitalism* (Heinemann, 1976) p 55 ff.
28. *Ibid.* p 84.
29. *Ibid.* p 84.
30. *Ibid.* pp 28, 29.
31. *Ibid.* p 171.
32. Christopher Lasch (1986) in *New Statesman*, 29 August (1980) *The Culture of Narcissism* (London: Abacus). Cited in Hoover and Plant, *Conservative Capitalism in Britain and the United States, op. cit.* p 234.
33. Alasdair MacIntyre, *After Virtue: A study in moral theory* (Duckworth, 1981) p 237.
34. *Ibid.* p 236.
35. *Ibid.* p 245.
36. Forrester, *Theology and Politics, op. cit.* p 144.
37. *Ibid.* p 145.
38. Lesslie Newbigin, *The Other Side of 1984* (World Council of Churches, 1983) p 56.
39. David Jenkins, 'The God of Freedom and the Freedom of God' (Hibbert Lecture, *Listener* April 18, (1985).
40. MacIntyre, *After Virtue, op. cit.* p 245.
41. Duncan B. Forrester, *Christianity and the Future of Welfare* (Epworth, 1985) p 87.
42. *Christian Faith and Political Hope: A Reply to E R Norman* (Epworth, 1979) p 139 ff.
43. *Faith in the City: Theological and Moral Challenges, op. cit.* p 47.
44. Gerard W. Hughes, *God of Surprises* (DLT, 1985)
45. Alan Ecclestone, *A Staircase for Silence* (DLT, 1977) p 88.

46. Forrester, *Theology and Politics, op. cit.* pp 165–6.
47. *Faith in the City of Birmingham* (Paternoster Press, 1988) p 127.
48. Ecclestone, *A Staircase for Silence, op. cit.* p 92.
49. Konrad Lorenz, *The Waning of Humaneness* (Unwin Hyman, 1988) p 177.
50. Board for Social Responsibility, *Changing Britain; Social Diversity and Moral Unity* (Church House publishing, 1987) p 23.
51. *Faith in the City, op. cit.* Recommendation 31. para. 12.53.
52. BSR, *Changing Britain, op. cit.* pp 23–4.
53. Atherton, *Faith in the Nation, op. cit.* Ch. 4.
54. *Ibid.* p 143.
55. Edward Norman, *Christianity and the World Order* (OUP, 1979) p 79.
56. Norman Mackenzie (editor), *Convictions*, MacGibbon and Kee 1958 p 118. Cited in Forrester, *Christianity and the Future of Welfare, op. cit.* p 87.

Epilogue

1. Robin Gill, *Beyond Decline: A challenge to the churches* (SCM Press, 1988) p 2.
2. *Ibid.* Ch 2.
3. *Ibid.* p 85. Also see Ch 3, p 42 ff.
4. Charles Elliott, *Praying the Kingdom* (DLT, 1985) p 127.
5. Gerard W. Hughes, *In Search of a Way* (DLT, 1986).